Learning to Listen to Palestine
A Personal Quest

Lani Lanchester

Foreword by Yohanna Katanacho

Copyright © 2024

All Rights Reserved

ISBN: 979-8-218-45044-1

Dedication

To my family for your lessons in love, truth, and hope. To my dad whom I love and miss so much. Especially to my mom who has journeyed with me learning about Palestine and encouraging me to keep learning.

To my Jordan family from Za'atari Village. Your love feeds my soul.

Acknowledgment

This book is wholly possible because of the kindness of a Palestinian friend who was there for me during many great losses over the last two years. He taught me of the resilient spirit of the Palestinian people when faced with seemingly unendurable crises. He taught me how prayer and the word of God gives a focus of hope. Moreover brotherly love endures all things.

As I struggled with new found information and sweeping doubt, bitterness, anger, frustration, I was often encouraged with words of how Jesus taught us to love and to bear challenges with faith. I have learned some of what it takes to be Palestinian. Deep enduring love.

My friend has been a source of clarifying information. He has helped lead me to reliable pastors, historians, and encouraging voices. He has checked my facts and filled in the holes in my story. Moreover, my friend has helped me with reviewing the manuscript and assuring my story is told with clarity.

I hope this book pays it forward in some meaningful way to the reader. If you struggle with sorrow, I have learned that sorrow is just love without an object. However, there are many people who need this love. Turning your focus outward to those who are enduring difficult things. This will make the world a better place.

About the Author

Lani Lanchester believes in taking every good opportunity, which has given her many great adventures. In her career, she has been an Agricultural Biologist, an IPM Program Coordinator, a pastry chef, a costume designer, a beekeeper, an Airbnb host, and currently, she is teaching high school science. She has taught biology, chemistry, physics, environmental science, engineering, architecture,  and health. Lani loves to garden, hike, and take long road trips, but she believes that we are best defined by our relationships.

Lani's the daughter of kind, Christian parents, the mother of two insightful talented women, and a sister, a friend, and a teacher, but her greatest love is Jesus. Lani leans on God's loving support through this complicated life. In response to God's loving kindness, Lani is called to a life of blessing others, speaking truth, seeking peace and loving life. Lani's greatest adventures are yet to happen.

Contents

Dedication i
Acknowledgment ii
About the Author iii
Suggested Additional Resources 1
Foreword by Yohanna Katanacho 2
Introduction 6
Chapter 1: Canceled 10
Chapter 2: Joppa, Wet Shoes, and a Treasure 14
Chapter 3: Walking in the Steps of Jesus 21
Chapter 4: Confronting 1948 25
Chapter 5: Baptismal Site? 32
Chapter 6: Living Stone 35
Chapter 7: Our Father, Pater Noster 42
Chapter 8: The Travels of Jesus 46
Chapter 9: The Destination the Way of Sorrows 50
Chapter 10: The Desert Blooms 56
Chapter 11: The Road to Za'atari 60
Chapter 12: Where is Jordan? 64
Chapter 13: Bedouin Hospitality 66
Chapter 14: Sama Albadia; In the Desert 70
Chapter 15: Weavers of Hope 74
Chapter 16: Learning to Listen 78
Chapter 17: Taking Sides 81
Chapter 18: Stuck Between Two Psychopaths 85
Chapter 19: "Olive You!" 90
Chapter 20: The Bottom-Line Weekend 96
Chapter 21: Switch 100
Chapter 22: The God Who Sees, the Who God Hears 105
Chapter 23: A Lesson in Humanity 110
Chapter 24: Forgiveness and Overcoming Bitterness 117
Appendix 122

Suggested Additional Resources

Companion Books: *The Book of Forgiveness* by Desmon Tutu. *The Land of Christ: A Palestinian* Cry by Yohanna Katanacho. *Finding Hagar God's Pursuit of a Runaway* by Michael F. Kuhn. *The Ethnic Cleansing of Palestine* by Ilan Pappe.

Companion Videos: *5 Broken Cameras* (2011) – A film by Emad Brunet concerning his Village Bil'in's struggle with Israeli illegal settlements in the West Bank encroaching on their village land. *Hebron Exposed, a Weapon of Life.* (2018) – A film by Tom Roberts. Palestinians arm themselves with cameras to curb the violence in Hebron.

Foreword by Yohanna Katanacho

I am indeed honored to write a foreword for the book *Learning to Listen to Palestine*. It provides a needed perspective for all people, regardless of their background. Lani Lanchester provides us with personal stories about her Christian journey as a servant of Christ. Her risky personal quest is to honor Christ, to be a peacemaker, to spread forgiveness, to walk where Jesus walked and where he is still walking. She wants to walk among Palestinians. In her Christian adventure, she encounters traumatized Middle Eastern people. She does not meet them as a tourist but as a follower of Christ who serves and listens. Yes, she listens and listens well. She humbly ministers to Palestinians in the West Bank, in Israel proper, in refugee camps, and in Jordan, as well as traumatized Syrians in Al Mafraq. Her book is full of encounters of listening well to Palestinians. She learns about their language and studies their culture. She joins their weddings and visits their homes. She eats their food. She becomes one with them.

In addition, the book deals with the painful current realities of the people of Gaza. I have heard of their pain firsthand from my friends Yousef Al Khoury and Shereen Awwad, who have relatives in Gaza. Both are teachers at Bethlehem Bible College. Some of their relatives were injured, and others were killed by an Israeli missile. I have also heard about the current realities of Gaza from Hanna, my student at Nazareth Evangelical College. His wife, Janet, was stuck in Gaza, but unlike many others, she was able to escape to Egypt.[1] The pain among Palestinians is loud, and the cry for help is deafening. Their cry for peace and justice is earsplitting. But could it be that Christian churches are deaf? Could it be that they are so biased to the extent that they are muting the voice of God and replacing biblical love with many merciless theologies?

I am reminded of John's call to the seven churches in the book of Revelation. He kept saying: "he who has an ear, let him hear what the Spirit says to the churches" (Rev 2: 7, 11, 17, 29; 3: 6, 13, 22). The sentence was repeated seven times. Each time, it addressed all the churches. God wants the global church to have a listening ear. The context is very gloomy. We encounter seven seals, seven trumpets, seven signs, and seven bowls of wrath. We encounter beasts, a dragon, and Babylon, the harlot. We encounter political persecution, religious persecution, hatred, injustices, heresies, and many forms of evil. Yet, God's advice is calling us to listen to the voice of the Spirit. The Spirit speaks through the apostle John, a persecuted follower of Christ suffering from political and religious oppression. God is still speaking today through the Scriptures as well as through the witness of his faithful servants who encounter a suffering world. The problem is not in finding the God who speaks; it is in having listening ears.

The church needs ears!! The blood of many innocent people is crying out like the blood of Abel (Gen 4: 10), but are we able to hear it?! Many people have been murdered. Can we hear the hunger for dignity and peace among Palestinians? God helped Paul to hear through a vision at night. He heard the Macedonian call: come over and help us (Acts 16: 9)! Lani has responded and is now calling others to listen to Palestinians. Listening to Palestinians does not mean muting Jewish voices. It is not listening from the perspective of a biased nationalism or a polarized political decision. Instead, it is a call to be a better listener and to have ears that are tuned to the voice of the Spirit, to Christlike love, to mercy, to justice, and to divine grace. It is the kind of listening that honors Christ and builds a better future for both Palestinians and Jews.

This kind of listening needs a divine spark. Lani is fanning the flames of love, not hate, of mercy, not cruelty, of inclusion, not exclusion, or xenophobia. Her book is a wakeup call for those who are willing to listen. We see in the Scriptures that God helped Samuel to hear his voice. Although Samuel did not understand in the first three times, he responded properly in the fourth time, saying: Speak, Lord, for Your servant hears (1 Sam 3: 9). Those who come with this attitude will hear God's heart through Lani's words. Furthermore, God helped Peter to hear. Ironically, he was in a trance, but God spoke to him three times, asking him to eat from a non-kosher food. Then, the Spirit informed him that three men were asking for him. God prepared his heart and gave him new ears to hear the call of Cornelius (Acts 10). Cornelius was his occupier and his political enemy. He was a Roman centurion. He represented everything that Peter hated. Cornelius was a religious enemy. He was a defiled gentile in a century in which idol worship was a global reality. Yet, God gave Peter ears to hear and a new heart to love those who are outside his comfort zone. Consequently, Cornelius became Peter's brother in Christ. This book will help you to discover new family members among Palestinians.

In short, listening is important. God's ears are always attentive to his people (Ps 34: 15). He heard the cries of those who are in need. He showed them mercy and love. He heard Ishmael and gave him water (Gen 21: 9-21). He heard the cry of Israel when they were oppressed in Egypt. He heard the world's need for salvation and died on the cross to save the people of Palestine and Israel. May we hear his voice through this book and spread love, not hate, for both Palestinians and Israelis. The first step in this journey of love is to start listening!

[1] https://www.christianitytoday.com/news/2023/november/flight-to-egypt-gaza-church-pastor-family-flee-porphyrius.html?fbclid=IwAR0kCkBeL_FEyrMPSqtL0bn79RaK72fk3v6RhQBBhTBBNn4mR1Jy-kgdu34

Introduction

There are three guides that helped me as I was on this quest, Learning to Listen to Palestine that I would like to introduce you to before you join me on my journey. Yohanna Katanacho a Palestinian theologian, Ilan Pappe a Jewish historian, and Desmond Tutu a South African peacemaker.

Yohanna Katanacho, a Palestinian Christian, is the Academic Dean of Nazareth Evangelical College in Israel and a Professor at Bethlehem Bible College in Palestine. His teaching and guidance helped me to clearly find the foundation on which to rebuild my understanding of Israel and Palestine. That foundation is Love.

He tells a story of when he was a young Christian, and God clearly instructed him to love his enemies. This was difficult. In the late 1980s, new Israeli law gave Israeli soldiers the authority to shoot a Palestinian if they did not promptly present their papers on request. One night, Yohanna Katanacho found himself looking down the barrels of three assault rifles aimed at his head.

Without thinking further, he raised his hand to his chest and said, "I have a heart here, that loves you." This shocked both the soldiers and him!

After he spoke to these soldiers for about 20 minutes, one soldier said, "I wish that all Palestinians were like you."

"No," Katanacho replied, "I wish that you were like me" (Katanacho 5).

After reading his work, I knew that I wanted to end my book with his voice, a Palestinian prayer. When I reached out to him, he gave me incredible encouragement. Moreover, as I was writing the book, and became frustrated by what I was learning, he responded to me as a pastor guiding his sheep, reminding me not to lose sight of Jesus and the mission of love.

Ilan Pappe, an Israeli Jew, is a professor with the College of Social Sciences and International Studies at the University of Exeter in the United Kingdom. Pappe grew up a typical Israeli from a Jewish town and went to Israeli schools. In the 1973 War, Pappe served in the Israel Defense Force (IDF).

He shares that when he studied history abroad, he met Palestinians as equals for the first time. Later as he was researching for his doctoral thesis in the early 1980s, he discovered information that had been unsealed regarding the early years of modern Israel and the Nakba, what the Palestinians call 1948 meaning the catastrophe.

Pappe reveals that he was cautious with this information at first, but after 30 years of research and study and several previous books, Pappe published a book that forced him to part from Israel for good, *The Ethnic Cleansing of Palestine* published 2006. This book gives a detailed account of what happened in 1947-1948.

Pappe has gathered information and multiple accounts like an archaeologist carefully piecing fragments together to reassemble broken pot shards. In the end, using Ben Gurion's journals, military orders, letters, and eye witness accounts, the events of

1947-1948 are uncovered clearly showing not only the events that occurred but also the names of those involved.

The first time I ever heard the term "Nakba" was from a Palestinian friend while visiting Israel. After this, I tried with very little success to uncover what happened to the Palestinians during those years. I could find many personal stories, but the viewpoint was very narrow. Discovering Ilan Pappe's research was monumental. I could not have succeeded in negotiating through this journey without his truth.

Desmond Tutu was the Archbishop of Cape Town, South Africa. Not only was he instrumental in bringing the Apartheid to an end, but he did something far more remarkable. He helped bring healing to South Africa.

I remember the news about South Africa in the 1980s. The incredible violence, oppression, and hate. *What a horrible place,* I thought. It was not until my dad died and I was under great pain, that my sister handed me *The Book of Forgiving* by Desmond Tutu.

I recommend everyone read it. I had no idea that South Africa had gone through this process of healing all those who had been scarred by the Apartheid. The book gave me hope and I could see the hope for Israel and Palestine.

That is why I wrote this book, for love, truth, and hope.

How to look at this book: Learning to Listen to Palestine is not a political book. Politics solves nothing, but it will call politics to the mat for dehumanizing people rather than uniting people. It is not a preaching book, but it is an honest reflection of my personal quest in learning to see the Palestinian people as I walk out my own faith with God. Ultimately my conclusions are that the Palestinian people need to be seen and cared for as our own neighbors and as our own brothers and sisters. They are family.

Chapter 1: Canceled

"Why am I going to Israel?" I wondered.

In December 2022, I decided to go to Hawaii alone to sit on a beach and cry.

Canceled. I had been canceled. I was shocked! My daughters had been steadily distancing themselves from me. I was trying to be patient. I understood, on an intellectual level, at least. They were in their early twenties, a time notoriously thick with confusion. The world had just emerged from the social upheaval of COVID-19, adding another layer to their already complex lives. They were also rekindling a relationship with their father, something I tried to support wholeheartedly.

Still, patience wore thin when communication dwindled. I hadn't heard from them in weeks. In an attempt to bridge the gap, I'd send little texts – a funny picture of the dog, an update on a project in the garden, maybe a sweet message reassuring them of my love. Even news about Papa and Nana (my aging parents). But there was not a single reply, not even a thumbs-up to acknowledge receipt. It felt like I was reaching out into a void.

When I went to the Verizon store to check on my account, my inquiry about my account revealed a detail I hadn't considered: their phones appeared to be inactive on my plan. A quick call to their father confirmed that, yes, they had new phones, but they did not want me to have their phone numbers. I was crushed and confused. How could this be?

Christmas was fast approaching, and I could not imagine spending Christmas explaining this to the rest of the family while they gave me advice on how to fix it. I craved a beach with rhythmic waves and the vast ocean far from everyone, where I could cry the way I needed to cry and feel what I could not avoid feeling.

In the meantime, I talked to a friend of mine. A Palestinian Christian from Nazareth, Israel, asked me, "Why would you go to Hawaii to be miserable? Come to Israel and walk in the steps of Jesus!" After praying about it, I really felt that this was what God wanted me to do.

As I planned, my caring father expressed concern for my safety. My dad was not so sure Americans were safe in Israel. I didn't plan on joining a tour group. Instead, I planned to travel alone with my little rental car, following an itinerary suggested by my Palestinian friend. To respect my dad, as I researched and planned my journey, I searched about Israel and Palestinian conflicts involving Americans. I was shocked to a halt by something I learned. This is when I read about Shireen Abu Akleh.

Everything I thought I knew about Israel was wrong.

Shireen Abu Akleh was almost exactly my age, 51 years old. She was born a Palestinian Christian in Jerusalem but earned her American citizenship. She became a field reporter for Al Jazeera to report on the conflicts between Israel and Palestinians. On

May 11, 2022, Shireen was targeted by the Israel Defense Force (IDF) and shot in the head. For a short time, the IDF denied this, but film footage documented what happened, and it was not possible to deny the truth. It was all so wrong.

I felt completely disoriented by learning of this event.

First, Israel: I had come to know this country as a haven of safety, one that people can count on for security protection. I thought the IDF's role was to protect and secure safety from hate. The IDF was supposed to protect and provide; instead, an innocent woman was dead, murdered by a sniper bullet.

Second, my Country: Shireen was a United States citizen! Where was the accountability? If a United States Citizen were mistreated in a foreign country, I would expect the United States' powerful resources to come to the aid of the US citizens - the consulate, the congress, or even the president - to put more effort into protecting our people abroad. Nothing was done. I wondered, "Well, a Democrat is in office." While I do not hold to either party, I had perceived Republicans as the ones who believed "Benjamin Netanyahu 'Bibi' could do no wrong." However, even President Biden did not demand accountability for the murder.

Third, the Press: She was a reporter targeted and shot in the head during a time of apparent peace. The crime was caught on film. She was merely there to watch and report on what the IDF was going to do in Jenin. There were many witnesses. She was an American citizen, and I knew nothing of this. If it were an American sports star who took illegal cannabis into Russia and was thrown in jail, we would hear about every detail repeatedly in every news report for weeks.

I asked my friend in Nazareth about Shireen. He only said quietly, "Yes, we all loved Shireen."

It's surreal when everything you thought you knew about something is instantly smashed. What was happening in Israel? I knew nothing. I understood nothing. I did not know what to think. I had no opinions. I was just lost.

I turned to God in my confusion. Should I even go? Is there something so wrong there that I should just learn to mind my own business? Sit on a beach in Hawaii and cry?

In my prayer, I clearly heard God tell me to go.

"Why?" I asked.

"To listen."

So, I went.

Chapter 2: Joppa, Wet Shoes, and a Treasure

On my first day in Israel, I stayed by the sea in Joppa. Here was my beach to cry on. Instead, in the morning, I was greeted by a misty rain and a beautiful rainbow over the Mediterranean Sea. My heart was filled with joy and peace.

My Palestinian friend had created a to-do list for Joppa. After an early breakfast and a gorgeous walk along the beach, I headed to the Church of Saint Peter. This church commemorates a world-turning event that I had read about in the Book of Acts.

In the Book of Acts, Chapter 10, the Bible tells the account of Peter while he was in Joppa. It was here that Peter had a marvelous vision from God. It was a pivotal point in the history of the church.

"Peter went up on the housetop to pray about the sixth hour. Then he became very hungry and wanted to eat, but while they made ready, he fell into a trance and saw heaven open and an object like a great sheet bound at the four corners, descending to him and let down to the earth. In it were all kinds of four-footed animals of the earth, wild beasts, creeping things, and birds of the air.

And a voice came to him, "Rise, Peter; kill and eat."

But Peter said, "Not so, Lord! For I have never eaten anything common or unclean."

And a voice spoke to him again the second time, "What God has cleansed you must not call common." This was done three times. And the object was taken up into heaven again.

Acts 10:9-16 NKJV

Peter explains this vision:

"God has shown me that I should not call any man common or unclean."

Acts 10:28 NKJV

Peter said,

"I see very clearly that God shows no favoritism. In every nation, he accepts those who fear him and do what is right...this is the message of Good News, that there is peace with God through Jesus Christ who is Lord of all."

Acts 10:34-36 NKJV

Another Vision

Just up the coast from Joppa in the City of Caesarea, Cornelius, a devout man who feared God and gave to the poor and prayed to God, had a vision. In his vision, an angel revealed to Cornelius the location of Peter in Joppa and that Peter had a message from God about what Cornelius must do. Acting on the vision, Cornelius sent messengers who found Peter precisely where instructed: at the house of Simon the Tanner. Accompanied by a group of fellow believers, Peter traveled to Caesarea with the messengers. There, Peter recounted the life and ministry of Jesus, from his baptism to death and resurrection. He emphasized that the prophets foretold forgiveness of sins for those who believe in Jesus.

Upon his return to Jerusalem, Peter had to report to the other Jewish believers in Jerusalem about what had happened. While hesitant at first, Peter told them the account of the vision from God, the appearance of an angel to Cornelius, and how the Holy Spirit came upon the new gentile believers. The Jews in Jerusalem responded:

"We can see that God has also given the Gentiles the privilege of repenting of their sins and receiving eternal life."

Acts 11:18 NKJV

Following the instructions, I found Saint Peter's Church but arrived too early. I wandered about the old city on the crooked roads that were barely alleyways for me. Coming from California, where the oldest things are weathered rocks and towering redwoods, this place was old. This, I realized, was the most ancient place I'd ever set foot in. People had been traipsing these worn alleys for thousands of years, and every space was still inhabited. I discovered the house marked as the site of Simon the Tanner's old home. Even this "new" building was centuries old.

Finally, as I made it back to the church, my shoes were soaked through. The lovely church was adorned with a nativity and Christmas tree set up inside for the holiday approaching. The frescos depicted the visions of Cornelius and Peter.

As I sat and prayed in this church. I reflected on the importance of what happened here. This was the very spot where God commanded Peter to share the message of salvation with the Gentiles. I found the place lovely, yet I didn't get the feeling I was searching for. Searching for significance, I reread the account in Acts 10-11, meditated on it, and offered a prayer of gratitude for my faith, and I was on my way.

Having checked off my to-do list early, I reluctantly headed back to the hotel; my feet were wet. I did not want to ruin my feet on the first day of my trip; I expected to do a lot more walking. Hoping to find a dry pair of shoes, I went the long way, walking through the shops in town. I wandered in and out of a few little gift shops with everything from carved olive wood Christmas ornaments to backgammon sets, scarves, t-shirts, and woven handbags, but no shoes.

Then, I stopped at a shop with beautifully carved antique furniture inlaid with mosaics of colored woods and mother-ofpearl. The shopkeeper, Yusuf, invited me in and started telling me stories about the antiquities of his shop.

It was an odd day. A warm rain was falling now, and no tourists were around. This was not tourist season, and this was not tourist weather. Except for the shopkeepers, there were no locals either. He inquired where I was from. I explained that I was from California, traveling on my own.

He asked, "Why are you here?"

I felt the Holy Spirit remind me, "I am here to listen." I said.

Yusuf looked me full in the face, then pulled up one of his lovely carved inlaid chairs for me and told me to wait a moment. He brought back hot tea. As we sat and discussed his shop, Yusuf showed me what he had been working on before I had come in. He had trays of silver jewelry that he was untangling and sorting. After COVID, a nearby silver shop went out of business, and he bought out the inventory. So, I sat there and helped him untangle chains as the rain drizzled outside.

It was a slow day. Not many tourists this time of year, and the drizzly rain kept most people inside. My new friend told me about the shop and his father, who taught him how to collect and repair the ancient treasures in his shop. He told me about his father, how he loved him and missed him since he died a year ago.

Other shopkeepers came around to meet me, and we swapped stories.

Yusuf told me stories of Joppa and of Israel. As he told the stories of his family, he explained that he and his family were

Palestinian Christians who could trace their roots in Joppa back to almost 2000 years.

Suddenly, I felt all the significance of this place, Biblical Joppa. I knew why the church felt so flat and one-dimensional to me. It was just a marker of a life long ago. But right here, in front of me, Yusuf was a direct descendant of what had occurred on the hill behind us overlooking the Mediterranean Sea.

Salvation is for all men, and it was for me. My friend and I talked about Jesus and the call on our lives to love each other.

Yusuf told me he was excited about his daughters coming for the holidays. He was a devoted husband and a father. He showed me pictures of those he loved the most.

But my listening was only beginning. As we sat there, drinking tea, sorting silver, and swapping stories about California and Israel, we heard a siren go by. "F*** the Israelis!" burst out of him. I didn't understand what just happened. Something had triggered him.

I knew from my experience of learning about Shireen that I knew nothing. So, I just said, "Tell me."

Yusuf went on to explain all that authorities were doing in Israel: beatings, murders, and destruction of Palestinian property. The IDF and the police were not trusted. I recalled what was happening back in the States; a police officer had put his knee on the neck of a handcuffed man during an arrest, but bystanders had caught it on video. The man died. The US was in an uproar about the incident. It was tearing our country apart, but this country was small, very small. How were they holding themselves together?

Later, after asking some questions and doing some Google searches, I learned there were very different laws for Palestinians and Jews. The protection of the police and the IDF (Israel Defense Force) was not for all people; it was only for Jews. I discovered that what held the country together seemed to be extreme oppression. Suddenly, I felt so disoriented and confused about the world.

When I asked my friend how I could pray for him, Yusuf said, "Pray for the safety of my family and peace."

After hours of sorting and conversations, my feet were dry. My mind was full, and my new friend gave me more things for my to-do list in Joppa. I bought three small pieces of silver from his shop. Two were little touristy trinkets that a Christian pilgrim would buy on a trip to the Holy Land, but one was a piece that I wanted. It felt so significant to this moment. It was a piece of Amber with an inclusion in a silver pendant setting. The silver was tarnished. The Amber was scratched, but I knew Amber was not a true stone; it was soft because it is a living stone made from the sap of a tree that has been fossilized.

The gem reminded me of the Palestinian Christians here in Joppa. Hardened by trials, scarred by rough circumstances around them, but a true treasure of history preserved within.

I left full of wonder, having met this rare treasure.

Chapter 3: Walking in the Steps of Jesus

If you can drive to Nazareth, Israel, during the Christmas Market, you can do anything!

This is a beautiful, amazing celebration of the Christian faith in Nazareth, but let me tell you, there are more cars than there are roads at this time of year. I stayed just one night in Nazareth, right in the old city and steps from the Christmas Market.

I did it with a smile, laughing and giggling at my predicament! Yet, taking on the impossible was possible. Eventually, I was parked with the help of a kind Palestinian man who stopped traffic and guided me into a tight spot. I walked this beautiful, warm December night down the streets of Nazareth and to the Church, the tree, and thousands of people and lights.

The next day, I met up with my friend. When I had met my friend years before, I nearly asked the typical question, *"When did your family convert to Christianity?"* Thankfully, I asked the more tactful question, "How long has your family been

Christian?" He is a Palestinian Christian who can trace their family roots back to the time of Jesus in Palestine. Most of my friends who travel to Israel, travel with Jewish guides and do not meet these native Christians who worship in these ancient churches that Westerners visit like relics of the past. But these Christians live and breathe the history of Christ and are almost part of the land itself.

When we met up for coffee, I was amazed listening to my friend move fluidly from English to Arabic to Hebrew. I learned that Palestinians native language is Arabic, but because of the British Mandate and the current ruling of the Holy Land by Israel, all three languages are taught in schools. Ove the millennia the language of the people changed many times. During the time of Christ, the most common languages were Aramaic, Greek and Latin. Each of these languages reflect a nation that conquered the Holy Land. In 638 AD the Holy Land was conquered by Caliph Umar. Arabic became the language of the ruling class and stayed that way for over a thousand years.

As we toured several churches that commemorated Jesus' ministry in the Galilee, he explained to me about the origins of these churches, their early history and their recent histories. It was amazing to hear the stories in the very places that they occurred.

I read from my little bible app, and I could see the care that the churches took to preserve the places and the stories for generations, but several times, something surprising and new and not so holy crept into the story. At the Church of the Multiplication of the Loaves and Fishes, I toured this early church built by Joseph of Palestine, a Jewish convert from the time of

Constantine. The ancient church had been rediscovered in the early 20th Century. Ornate mosaic floors with depictions of the local wild life were restored. 5th Century mosaic tiles carefully assembled from ancient floors and new pieces as well However, recent history shows something terribly wrong.

In 2015, arsonists set the church on fire. Hateful graffiti was sprayed on the walls. The church never closed but was set to work to repair the damage, yet Israeli news reported that the church had closed. The arsonists were said to be Jewish radicals.

I did a Google search on Church burnings in Israel. This is not rare, and these occurrences are increasing.

This surprised me and confused me. I had thought that Christians were great supporters of the Jews and Jews were great supporters of Christians. Christians send billions of dollars to Israel every year to help support the elderly, plant trees and help desperate people make aliyah. Our churches prayed for Israel, but in Israel, the church is under persecution.

Perplexingly, this is not a new phenomenon. In an article from 2017 from Haaretz News, the author reports, "Over 50 Christian and Muslim sites have been vandalized in Israel and in the West Bank since 2009" (Berger). Few of these incidents are investigated. Convictions are rare. Again, I am bewildered. How did we not know this?

However, Christian leaders from the Church of the Multiplication believe in miracles. In this church the small blessing of five loaves of bread and two fish is remembered. This small gift was shared among five thousand people. The multitude ate and were filled and twelve baskets full of fragments remained. Today Palestinian Priest Father Mattias declares, "There's a second fire- the fire of solidarity and love,....Jewish friends have been showing up here for the past six months to offer their support and to assure us that the extremists will not win"(Lawler).

This small blessing of support for Father Mattias, I pray in Jesus' name that this support will reach the multitudes in all the Holy Land.

Chapter 4: Confronting 1948

Riding up the winding road to the Church of the Beatitudes, my friend was teaching me about all the landscape that was spreading before us. In one direction is the Sea of Galilee, in another is the Golan Heights, and in another is the Jordan Valley. All my life, I had heard these names in Bible stories and occasionally in the news. He mentioned 1948, and I, in my naivete, said, "There must have been something righteous about 1948."

The car stopped, and in an angry, frustrated voice, he said, "Righteous?! 530 Arab villages were destroyed. They killed men, women and children. There were massacres, rapes, 750,000 people were forced out of their homes. The Jews now plant trees over these destroyed villages to cover the evidence!"

I had never heard this before. None of this. This was Earth-shaking to me. "I have never heard this. Please tell me." I asked, but he was angry. I heard the Spirit remind me to listen. I heard his anger, his disappointment, and how alone it must feel for large portions of the population to be so ignorant of this severe trauma of his people and family.

Earlier, he had driven me by a house and explained that it had once been an ancestral home but had been lost in 1948. How could I understand this?

Growing up, there was this exciting mysticism about Israel. We had a Christian home full of music, Bible study, and Church on Sundays and Wednesdays. We grew to love God and the stories of the Bible.

Moses, David & Goliath, and the Psalms of David were precious to us. We read them, sang them, and meditated on them. We memorized sections of the Bible, especially the words of Jesus. Reading about Jesus walking from village to village with miracles performed at the different sites in Israel created a longing for a connection to the land.

Jesus' simple yet profound teachings changed the world, the parables that he taught that we still chew on today, trying to digest all the wisdom imparted; these things were the deep roots of my life. Among them woven in was Israel, modern Israel. The way we were raised was that this was a *modern miracle*. God had gathered the Jewish diaspora from around the world to escape persecution in the land of Israel. Despite the rocky start of nearly being destroyed from its inception, they survived surrounded by nations that hated them. We would hear repeated God's promise:

"And I will make you a great nation, and I will bless you, and make your name great; and you shall be a blessing: And I will bless them that bless you, and curse him that curse you; and in you shall all families of the earth be blessed."

Genesis 3:2-3 NKJV

Christian Zionism is a force that drives much of our very good population of people in a direction with blinders so that we do not see the landscape around us. We do not see the whole truth. For the truth, we must listen to those who speak another language.

We must love someone from another culture. We must hear the stories that shake our world. People who love God and who grew up worshiping, praying, and seeking to do good are guided by blinders. It was honestly difficult for me to hear what Palestinians have to say.

The influence of Zionism on me and the Genesis 12 scripture above is akin to rubbing the tummy of a magic golden idol. I was led to believe that in blessing Israel, I will be blessed, and cursing Israel, you will be cursed. I learned that Genesis 12 has been mistranslated. Yohanna Katanacho explains the problem with the Genesis 12 promise.

The text doesn't say to Abram, 'You shall be a blessing.' The Hebrew text gives a command, 'Be a blessing.' Therefore, in the name of bad translation, people justify unconditional support for Israel (Kaylor and Harmon 2015). Be a blessing, and I will bless them that bless you and curse them that curse you. It makes so much more sense. The blessing is conditional on behavior.

I did some reading after this to try to learn for myself what actually happened. To be honest, it was a very skeptical reading. As I said before, Christian Zionism has deep roots, and pulling up the lies was earth-shaking.

To the Palestinian people, the 1948 war of Independence is known as Nakba, the Catastrophe. I had never heard of this term before this trip. More than 500 villages and cities were destroyed. Nearly a million people were displaced. When you look for how many people were killed, it is vague. "Dozens of massacres." This plural dozen can mean so many things. How many people were killed in these massacres? Who was it?

Why is it so vague? Because it is difficult to learn. While there are archaeological digs to uncover the distant past of Biblical times, 1948 had many layers of heaping rubble of propaganda, rumors, and lies. It would take me some time to dig through what was true and what was not just to begin to understand. I am now committed to continuing to learn what is true.

Ilan Pappe, an Israeli historian, explains in his 2006 book *The Ethnic Cleansing of Palestine,* "It is indeed hard to understand, and for that matter to explain, why a crime that was perpetrated in modern times and at a juncture in history that called for foreign reporters and UN observers to be present, should have been so totally ignored. And yet, there is no denying that the ethnic cleansing of 1948 has been eradicated almost totally from the collective global memory and erased from the world's conscience. Imagine that not so long ago, in any given country you are familiar with, half of the entire population had been forcibly expelled within a year, half of its villages and towns wiped out, leaving behind only rubble and stones. Imagine now the possibility that somehow this act will never make it into the history books and that all diplomatic efforts to solve the conflict will totally sideline, if not ignore, this catastrophic event" (Pappe 9).

I searched for a year for information about the Nakba. I could hear stories from Palestinian families that I spoke with who were glad to tell their story. Tragic as these were, this gave me a very limited point of view.

My breakthrough was when I discovered Ilan Pappe, a Jewish Historian. Ilan Pappe is a rare investigator of the Nakba of 1948. He has sifted through the rubble of documentation, scattered stories of survivors and perpetrators like an archaeologist sifting for potshards. But he is an Israeli, with a typical Israeli upbringing in an all-Jewish city. He went to Israeli schools and served in the IDF during the 1973 War. However, in the 1980's, Pappe studied the original documents from 1948 that were unsealed in 1978. Pappe cautiously at first revealed what the found, but in 2006 he published a book that forced him to leave Israel for good, *The Ethnic Cleansing of Palestine*. This book tediously details all the events and participants of the Nakba, that did not start in 1948, but began in 1947.

The version of 1948 that I had known was called the Israel War of Independence. In this version, the Arab League made up of seven Arab armies, invaded the fledgling country of Israel. Israel was defended by the Hagana (which means defense in Hebrew) and the Irgun Stern Gang a violent and unrestrained terrorist organization. Much blame was put on evil deeds of that year on the Irgun Stern Gang. However, once I discovered Pappe's research on 1947-1948, an entirely different picture emerges.

Operation for the War of Independence, or we should call it here, the Nakba, began in 1947. Zionist forces planned years in advance. The plan was called Plan Dalet. All Palestinian villages and cities were scouted. Relationships were recorded. Lists of people who would be arrested and who would be silenced permanently were created.

Then ahead of May 15, 1948, the day the British Mandate was to end and the UN Resolution that would divide Palestine into a Palestinian state and a Zionist state would go into effect, Jewish forces began their plan. It began in areas that the British left unguarded with a few villages being ethnically cleansed (meaning the removal of all Arabs) in February and culminated in April with the cleansing of Haifa, Jaffa, Safad, Beisan, Acre, and Western Jerusalem. Pappe explains that the largest urban centers had been "ethnically cleansed" from Arabs before May 15, 1948, and before the Arab League engaged in the defense of Palestine too little and too late with poor organization.

By the time the Arab League had joined the fight, the organization of the Zionist forces were sweeping the land. 530 villages were systematically destroyed. Witness stories of the Nakba are now passed down. Here is one story Pappe relates in his book of these oral histories, "My maternal grandmother was a teenager when Israeli troops entered Bassa and ordered all the young men to be lined up and executed in front of one of the churches. My grandmother watched as two of her brothers, one 21, the other 22 and recently married, were executed by the Haganah" (Pappe Ethnic Cleansing 142).

One account that I found most amazing was the account of the survival of Nazareth. In 1948, the commander of the Israeli Army's Seventh Armored Brigade, Ben Dunkleman, disobeyed orders to expel residents of Nazareth and accepted their surrender (Cook).

From this article, I learned what the policy of the Israeli Army was that left little to no paper trail. Village by village, peaceful civilians were forced from their homes.

"Some 750,000 Palestinians – out of 900,000 living inside the borders of what was to become the new Jewish state – were forced out and refused the right to return. In fact, the expulsion rate was far higher than the ostensible 80 percent figure. Under pressure from the Vatican, Israel allowed many Christian refugees back; it did a land swap with Jordan in 1949 that brought more than 30,000 Palestinians into the new state, and many Palestinian refugees managed to sneak back to surviving communities like Nazareth and blend in with the local population in preparation for what they hoped would be their return to their villages" (Cook).

The land of Israel holds my heart. My identity and intimacy with God are closely related to these stories and these places, and I still don't think that this is wrong. However, I need to take off the blinders to see and open my ears to hear what is really there.

Chapter 5: Baptismal Site?

My friend had given me directions to drive to the Baptismal Site of Jesus on the Jordan River. I drove pass a military checkpoint where a soldier checked my passport. I crossed a span of desolate land. I passed a monastery that seemed deserted. When I got to the Baptismal Site, I found a concrete complex of bus parking, gift shops, concrete steps, concrete pavilions, changing rooms, lockers and Israeli flags.

I made my way pass all this and walked past IDF soldiers with M-16 assault rifles and large warning signs in many languages warning tourists not to leave the complex because of the landmines surrounding the complex and following the Jordan River. This was a military zone.

The Jordan River was a small, murky, green-brown creek lined with willows, palms, and reeds. Wooden steps led down to the small stream that I could easily walk across, except that I might be shot or at least for sure arrested. This felt wrong. I was here looking for the footsteps of Jesus, and I found fear and trouble, not peace.

On the far side of the river (it's not that far), I saw what seemed to be a peaceful place. A wooden deck with a wooden pergola to offer shade to guests and just a few steps to the river. Behind this, I could see many trees and a church a short walk away. Behind this, I could see more small churches. On the deck was a flag.

The concrete was crowded with Christian pilgrims going in groups to the water with their religious guides. I stood back and watched and waited for a moment to walk to the river myself. When the moment came, two Muslim women and I stood on the platform, taking pictures. I asked them about the flag. It looked like the Palestinian flag. "That is the Jordan flag." They explained. "Jordan is Palestine." They explained that the flag was the same, except the Jordanian flag had a star.

Feeling a longing to see that church, "What is over there?" I asked.

"You can visit the churches if you go from the Jordan side." They explained.

I spent some time there reading from my Bible app. This was the location where Joshua led the children of Israel across the Jordan to the Promised Land. This was possibly near where Elijah spent three and a half years in exile while God withheld rain from Israel due to Israel's worship of Baal. This is where John the

Baptist performed his ministry, and this is where Jesus began his ministry, and God proclaimed from heaven, "This is my beloved son, in whom I am well pleased." This has always been a site of world-changing events, but to experience it, I would need to go to Jordan.

Much later, I learned that this was the first time that I entered Palestine. During the Oslo Accords, the West Bank was divided into three areas called A, B, and C. This was Area C, an area completely under Israeli military jurisdiction. The Oslo Accords had promised to slowly transfer this land to the control of the Palestinian jurisdiction with options of land swaps. This did not happen. Ariel Sharon, an advocate for this peace plan, was shot. The plan was not followed. Instead, Area A and Area B became isolated, fragmented, and encroached by illegal settlements paid for by the state of Israel and Zionist organizations from the United States.

Chapter 6: Living Stone

One of my students asked me, "Ms. Lanchester, did you celebrate Christmas?" I have never told them my faith, but I have reassured my Muslim and Christian students as I teach them many weeks of Evolution in my Biology class that I will teach them both the strengths and the weaknesses of the Theory of Evolution. They highly suspect me of being a creationist, but I just smile and tell them that I cannot tell them my beliefs. So, this was a loaded question. A few of the boys wanted to know if I was Christian or if I was Jewish.

"I did celebrate Christmas this year!" I declared, "In Palestine! I went to Bethlehem."

"Oh, that's cool." One of the boys said with respect. Later in the lab, these boys called me to their conversation. "Miss, who do you think is at fault? Israel or Palestine?"

"Honestly?" They nodded at me to encourage an answer. "Honestly, I would like to slap both sides, but that would just cause more hate and fear. We need to learn to love each other."

You cannot drive from Israel to Bethlehem, Palestine in a rented car. So, I hired a cab driver to take me to Bethlehem from Jerusalem. My Palestinian friend has given me a to-do list of places I should visit and things that I should look for in the churches and gardens around the churches. My driver, Mohammed, was such a kind man and asked me what I knew about Bethlehem, and what I wanted to see. I told him I knew very little and that I wanted to listen to people.

I did not understand about the walls between Israel and Palestine. I did not understand the refugee camps, so he told me about the area and the people. 780,000 Palestinians were expelled in 1948 when 530 Palestinian villages were destroyed. Today there are 58 refugee camps in Palestine, Jordan, Syria, and Lebanon. Three refugee camps are in Bethlehem.

My driver took me to the Aida Refugee camp where he introduced me to his friend. I had tea with a lovely Palestinian woman. She told me about being relocated to this small home and how she turned a cement yard into a small paradise by gathering bits of soil where she could, as well as making compost from leftover vegetable peelings. She collected cuttings and seeds. She had citrus, herbs, vegetables, flowers, and grape vines in her garden. She showed me pictures of the home that her family lost in 1948. A drawing of a Palestinian style home surrounded by fruit trees and olive orchards. I could see from the artwork the lushness of her garden in the refugee camp. This was a small sample of the lush gardens that her family had kept in their estate. Surrounding the edge of the frame beautiful Arabic calligraphy told the story of their home. This Muslim woman told me about the struggle to hold a family together in the small home in the camp, and a beautiful will to survive and thrive in the space that she was allowed. We had a lovely visit. Her peace and resilience left a changing mark on my soul.

Then, my guide took me to a shop to have lunch with some of the locals who lived in the camp. The shop had paintings on the walls of many more farms. Beautiful Arabic calligraphy framed the paintings. They asked why I was there, traveling by myself. I told them that I was there to listen. So, the residents began showing me the paintings and explaining that these were their ancestral homes and that they had lost some in 1948 and some in 1967.

I had honestly never considered civilians who lost homes and farms in these wars. My own family had a small family farm that held our family memories and much of our spirit.

The trees we planted and the family events that we had there were precious. These people had lost so much. I felt so tired suddenly under the weight of this burden.

Mohammed also took me to a factory where the Palestinian artists carved olive wood into beautiful treasures that tourists purchased and took all over the world. This Christian family brought out coffee and baklava sweets and showed me some of the pieces that they had made recently. I gave some news about California, but mostly I listened. They told me about the slow sales and learning to sell by mail order. But mostly, they were concerned about peace. Their children were relocating to other countries around the world to escape the oppression.

"How can I pray for you?" I asked.

"Pray for the peace of Jerusalem." They said seriously.

I toured several churches after this, but it was in the Grotto behind the Shepherds' Field Church that I sat and processed what I was learning to hear. I wrote out scriptures that came to my mind and the impressions that I felt in this ancient cave.

The stones, the ancient churches built on other ancient churches, were just stones. Markers of something past, ancient remains of Jesus' birthplace in this place long ago. The roof of the cave was covered in soot. Some of the soot could have been from the time of the shepherds, but most of the thick black soot was from two millennia of prayer candles lit as pilgrims like myself tried to imagine this place thousands of years ago.

But I found Living Stones, a family of Palestinian Christians in Bethlehem, a Palestinian Christian community in Nazareth, and Palestinian Christians in Joppa. The heart of the living stones that I have met is love. There are layers of soot on the outside, showing how the world has treated them, but inside is Jesus, still alive and showing the love of Jesus in this Holy Land.

In my continued prayer for the Palestinian people in Bethlehem and in the concentration camps there, I read about the changes in Bethlehem. In the 1920's Bethlehem was 80% Christian. Many of these people from this once small community could trace their roots back to the time of Jesus, many were likely descendants of the shepherds who witnessed the proclamation of the angels and finding Mary and Joseph in this cave with the baby Jesus lying in the manger.

However, this community has been crammed with displaced Palestinians who lost their farms and land to a systematic ethnic cleansing of 1948 and further displacement in 1967. Today due to the many refugees living in Bethlehem and the emigration of

Christians from Bethlehem, the percentage of Christians is just 20% of the population.

Despite this change in demographics within Bethlehem, Christian Palestinians and Muslim Palestinians are not against each other. A wall of separation between Palestine and Israel built in 2002 now characterizes the struggles of the Palestinians in Bethlehem with the Zionist regime of Israel.

Many Palestinians from the refugee camp still held hope of returning to their homes. The Christians carried their hope in their hearts. All waited.

"Hope deferred makes the heart sick, but when the desire comes, it is a tree of life." Proverbs 13:12 NKJV

As I continue my search to the greater extent of Israel and Palestine, I learn that in the 1920's, Christians were about 9-10% of the population, but today the current figures of Christians in all Israel and Palestine are less than 2%. According to most Christian missionary organizations this would indicate that the Holy Land, the land of Christ, is unreached by the Gospel.

However, the Christian Church in the Holy Land is not inactive or ineffective. I came across a document in a search called *Kairos*

Palestine. In this document, the Patriarchs and the heads of the churches lay out their hope for the Holy Land.

"Hope within us means first and foremost our faith in God and secondly our expectation, despite everything, for a better future. Thirdly, it means not chasing after illusions - we realize that release is not close at hand. Hope is the capacity to see God in the midst of trouble, and to be co-workers with the Holy Spirit who is dwelling in us. From this vision derives the strength to be steadfast, remain firm and work to change the reality in which we find ourselves. Hope means not giving in to evil but rather standing up to it and continuing to resist it. We see nothing in the present or future except ruin and destruction. We see the upper hand of the strong, the growing orientation towards racist separation, and the imposition of laws that deny our existence and our dignity. We see confusion and division in the Palestinian position. If, despite all this, we do resist this reality today and work hard, perhaps the destruction that looms on the horizon may not come upon us."

Kairos 9-10

I understood the request of my new Palestinian friends, "Pray for the peace of Jerusalem." Jerusalem is a city of Christians, Muslims, and Jews. Peace is the greatest gift for all of these religions, and to do this, we need love and forgiveness.

Chapter 7: Our Father, Pater Noster

Climbing to the top of the Mount of Olives is quite the hike. Jesus and his disciples must have been in pretty good shape! Today, on the Mount of Olives, there are several churches. Pater Noster, which means "Our Father," has been in the back of my mind and often in the front of my mind ever since climbing that mountain.

As I wound through the ancient olive orchard, a sense of wonder and expectation grew.

Some of these trees were here when Jesus camped and taught here. They are a living monument, but surprisingly to me, inside, there was a greater living monument. This church marks the spot where Jesus taught his disciples how to pray. The reference can be found in Luke 11:

"And it came to pass that, as he was praying in a certain place, when he ceased, one of his disciples said to him, Lord, teach us to pray, as John also taught his disciples.

And he said unto them, When you pray, say,

Our Father in heaven, Hallowed be your name.

Your kingdom come;

Your will be done, on earth as it is in Heaven.

Give us day by day our daily bread.

And forgive us our sins; for we also forgive everyone that is indebted to us.

And lead us not into temptation; but deliver us from the evil one."

Luke 11:1-4 NKJV

As I walk through the church, I see large, beautiful ceramic plaques with translations of the Lord's Prayer. The walls are covered in the Lord's Prayer in 172 languages throughout this church.

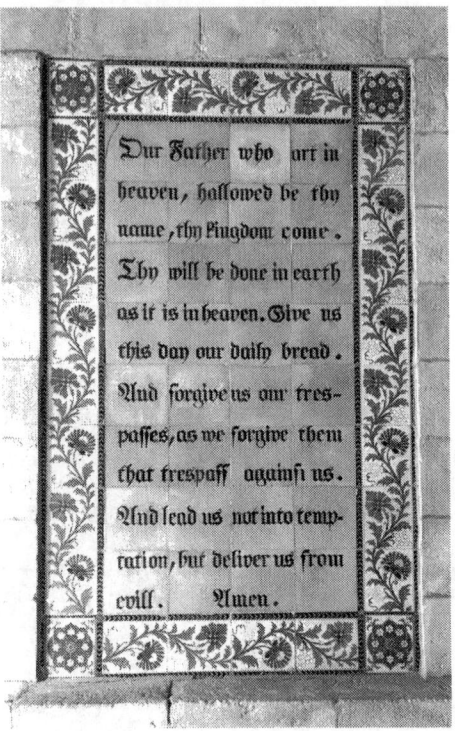

Tired from my climb, I sat on a bench and wrote out the prayer in my journal. I meditated on this prayer as I wrote it out. Maybe climbing up that steep hill affected my imagination, but it occurred to me that this place was the very antithesis of the Tower of Babel. At the Tower of Babel, man had become like a god to himself, the language was confused, and mankind was scattered and divided into many nations. Here, the language is brought together for all in one prayer, mankind is united as one family, and the one God is our Father.

Here on this hill, Jesus taught one prayer for all.

"Our Father in heaven" we have one father. We are one family. We are one people. *"Your kingdom come. Your will be*

done on earth as it is in Heaven." In Heaven, there is one nation. We are not divided by skin color, language, or culture. We are one people with one Father and with one king. Nationalism has no place in the Kingdom of God, the *family* of God.

"Give us day by day our daily bread." We rely on the same father for our daily needs.

"And forgive us our sins; for we also forgive everyone that is indebted to us." Forgiveness is essential to God's plan. The hate and the fear that divide us and keep us hurting each other find their end as we seek to follow Jesus.

"And lead us not into temptation, but deliver us from the evil one." And here is a shocker: we have one enemy, and it is not each other. It is Satan.

At one time, I believed that God was a Zionist and that He was calling the Jews back to the land. At the heart of Zionism is nationalism, the idea that God values the nation of Israel over all other nations. However, as I had meditated and examined this premise, I knew that it was not right. Finding the truth was difficult, but not so difficult here.

I recalled the vision that Jesus had sent Peter in Joppa. I pondered the vision that Jesus blinded Saul with on the Road to Damascus. I cannot see any Zionism in Jesus' teaching. I can only see the Lord's Prayer. We are united in God's Kingdom. This is not replacement theology. Through *Jesus*, all families of the world are blessed. Through this *prayer*, all families in the world are blessed.

Chapter 8: The Travels of Jesus

Enjoying the unseasonably warm weather for December, I drove with the windows down and music blasting and singing. I saw road signs for places like Jericho, the Dead Sea, Mount Carmel, Nazareth, the Sea of Galilee, En Gedi, Qumran, and Jerusalem. I covered the ground quickly. No drive was more than 45 minutes. Always, there was more to stop and see, but the most amazing part of the adventure was listening to the people. I wish I could have taken it at a slower pace rather than zooming pass.

This made me consider Jesus' travel. I have often been perplexed at Jesus' three-year ministry. He traveled back and forth, and this way and that, across Judea, Samaria, Galilee, Idumea, Perea, Decapolis, Gaulanitis, Syria, and Phoenicia like he owned them. He obviously did not have a travel guide making an itinerary, or a campaign director or a military strategist, but he was on a mission. On foot or maybe on a donkey, Jesus' pace was slower. Today we just zoom pass needy people on the street. In California, I zoom down Highway 99 several times a week pass the same homeless camps, pass the same people. This zipping pass dehumanizes them and their plight. I don't know their names, their story, or their needs. Jesus traveled on the ground at their pace, slowing for people, making eye contact, and hearing their plea. Jesus listened to their suffering.

I resonate with the Buddhist saying, *"All life is suffering."* I experience students with trauma often. Here on this trip launched by suffering of broken relationships, I contemplate how the older I get, the more suffering I carry.

Not just aches and pains in my body but lost loved ones to old age. Friends my age lost to cancer. I lost a young cousin to a tragic car accident. His mom was never the same after that. Then there are the abusive behaviors of people that cause horrible trauma, poverty, fear, loneliness, and neglect. Recently, a close friend of mine said, "I will never believe in God after what we are witnessing."

I had to agree with her sentiment, but I hold on to hope, "yes, all life is suffering, unless there is something more." Jesus came and walked among our suffering.

"Then it happened, as He was coming near Jericho, that a certain blind man sat by the road begging. And hearing a multitude passing by, he asked what it meant.

So, they told him that Jesus of Nazareth was passing by.

And he cried out, saying, "Jesus, Son of David, have mercy on me!"

Then those who went before warned him that he should be quiet, but he cried out all the more, "Son of David, have mercy on me!"

So, Jesus stood still and commanded him to be brought to Him. And when he had come near, He asked him, saying, "What do you want Me to do for you?" He said, "Lord, that I may receive my sight."

Then Jesus said to him, "Receive your sight; your faith has made you well. And immediately, he received his sight and followed Him, glorifying God. And all the people, when they saw it, gave praise to God." Luke 18:35-43 NKJV

Mark 1:40-45	Jesus heals a leper	Galilee
Matt 8:5-13	Jesus heals the centurion's servant	Capernaum, Galilee
Mark 5:1-20	Jesus casts out demons	Gadara, Decapolis
Luke 8:43-48	Jesus heals a woman with issue of blood for 12 years	In a village on the shore of Galilee
Luke 8: 40-56	Jesus raises 12 years old girl to life	In a village on the shore of Galilee
Mark 7:24-30	Jesus casts out a demon from a young girl	Tyre, Phoenicia
Mark 7: 31-37	Jesus heals a deaf-mute	Sea of Galilee, Decapolis
Luke 7:11-15	Jesus raises a mother's son from the dead	Nain, Galilee
Mark 8:22-26	Jesus heals a blind man	Bethsaida, Gaulanitis
Mark 9:14-29	Jesus heals a demon-possessed boy	Caesarea Philippi, Gaulanitis
Mark 10:46-52	Jesus heals blind-Bartimaeus	Jericho, Judea
Luke 17:11-19	Jesus heals ten lepers	Village in Samaria

This scene happened numerous times as Jesus traveled place by place.

These are just a few of Jesus' journeys in which people's needs were met wherever he roamed. The Gospels record that everywhere he went, he healed all the sicknesses of the people. Jesus also sent his disciples traveling to heal the sick and to preach. Jesus forgave their sins and taught them how to live. Jesus dominated the land with compassion.

Jesus asks, "What do you want me to do for you?"

Jesus connected with all this suffering as he traveled the land. The greatest suffering we endure is our separation from God. The meaninglessness of life without our creator drives us to do so much doing. We were created for this relationship, but we cannot repair this relationship.

Chapter 9: The Destination the Way of Sorrows

My pulse raced as I saw the road sign in Hebrew, Arabic, and English: Jerusalem! This was the culmination of my travels. In Jesus' journey, this was always his destination.

Jesus explained this plainly that the suffering he would endure, rejection by the elders, chief priests and teachers of the law, and that he must be killed and after three days rise again. The disciples were confused about this. Why would God ever want Jesus to die? How can death be his obedient destination after so much good that he had done in the land and after centuries of waiting for the Messiah?

I arrived in Old City Jerusalem after dark and entered through the New Gate into the Christian Quarter. Christmas lights adorned the street and alley. Christmas music played and vendors set up booths selling little handmade gifts, hot chocolate, sweets, soups, and breads. I visited with these Palestinian families. I bought a pair of earrings made by a mother and daughter. I asked a boy which soup was the best. All the tables and chairs were full, so I joined some Palestinian families sitting on the sidewalk.

I learned as I sat there that this was the Christian Quarter of the Old City and had been continuously inhabited by Palestinian Christians from the time Sultan Suleiman the Magnificent conquered Jerusalem and ordered the walls to be rebuilt. An Armenian Palestinian complete this story for me the next day. He guided me down the dividing line between the Quarters of the Old City. He explained the four Quarters of the Old City, Jewish Quarter, the Muslim Quarter, the Christian Quarter, and the Armenian Quarter (also Christian), was established by Sultan Suleiman the Great to preserve the peaceful coexistence of all the religions of Abraham. This peace persisted for over 400 years.

In the Jerusalem Christian Market that night, I guess I could not stop smiling, because after a few minutes a Jewish couple stopped to talk to me. "We saw you at the hotel. You are just glowing with happiness; we want to know why?"

I told them about my travels learning about the places that I had read in the Bible, and I never expected to be in Old City Jerusalem. They gave me their phone numbers and invited that if I was ever in Tel Aviv that I must visit them.

The next day I continued the path of Jesus, the destination of his journeys the Via Dolorosa, the "Way of Sorrow". My Palestinian friend had warned me that I didn't need a pushy guide, just a little booklet that I could buy to guide me through the 14 stations of the Via Dolorosa. So, I politely avoided many guides and found my little English booklet that I bought for 5 shekels.

I walked the path of Jesus, but not the final path of Jesus. From his arrest, condemnation, lashings, humiliation to his crucifixion lasted from around 2 AM to 9 AM. I never knew how shockingly fast this happened. The trumped-up charges were forced through quickly.

I sat in a cold basement for a while that had been used for a jail. Possibly, Jesus and Barabas had been kept here together. As I sat there some children had been let out of school. I could hear them on the street running and playing, but I can imagine Jesus heard the crowds outside having turned on him, rioting outside.

The streets were far narrower than I ever imagined. They are not wider than a high school hallway in many places.

Jesus must have dragged his cross at first through a military area and then into the markets. People crowded, preparing food, selling clothing, spices, things for the Passover. Blood thirsty spectators watched in the mob. Jesus' mother waited for him in the crowd.

Jesus stumbles trying to make a turn. After a night of beatings, judging and ridicule, this strong man who had walked the length and breadth of the land, struggled to make it the last few steps of his journey. Simon of Cyrene takes up the cross for Jesus. Twice more Jesus falls. He is breaking, but he turns to console the women who mourn for him.

"Daughters of Jerusalem do not weep for me; weep for yourselves and for your children. For the time will come when you will say, 'Blesses are the barren women, the wombs that never bore and the breasts that never nursed.' Then they will say to the mountains, 'Fall on us!' And to the hills, 'Cover us!' For if men do

these things when the tree is green, what will happen when it is dry?" Luke 23:28-31 NKJV

Jesus was led to Golgotha where they crucified him. He never fought it. Not at his arrest, not in the sham trial, not before Pilot, never. I have heard arguments about "the Jews who killed Jesus" or "the Romans killed Jesus," but this is underestimating what happened here. This was Jesus' destination the whole time.

Just as Abraham took his son Isaac possibly to this same spot and prepared his son as a sacrifice out of obedience to God, God sent his son Jesus to the cross and Jesus went willingly.

He died for us. This world is full of suffering because of sin. There was nothing we could do to fix it. All life is suffering, unless there is something more. There is more:

"For when we were still without strength, in due time Christ died for the ungodly. For scarcely for a righteous man will one die; yet perhaps for a good man someone would even dare to die. But God demonstrates his His own love toward us, in that while we were still sinners, Christ died for us. Much more then, having now been justified by His blood, we shall be saved from wrath through Him. For if when we were enemies we were reconciled to God through the death of His Son, much more, having been reconciled, we shall be saved by his life. And not only that, but we also rejoice in God through our Lord Jesus Christ, through whom we have now received the reconciliation." Romans 5:6-11

I entered the Church of the Holy Sepulchre. Inside is an overwhelming of the senses from gilded glory of 1500 years of worshipers that adorned the walls, powerful incense, crusader crosses carved into the plaster, paintings, icons, many pilgrims, and tractors. Yes, in the middle of the enormous church, renovations were underway with beeping bobcat tractors, temporary walls, and warning signs.

I stood bewildered with three women wearing hijabs. One was from France; two others were from Morocco. They were trying to understand what the mural in front of us was showing. Together we pieced together the illustration's meaning. The painting depicted mostly women gathered around the body of Jesus laid on the ground, but there was a gray hared man at Jesus' feet. "Who is this" they wondered. "Is it Moses, or a disciple?"

We went through the account of Jesus' death together to identify who this might be. "It cannot be a disciple. They were too young. That younger man over there is probably the disciple John." I speculated. Finally, I remembered Joseph of Arimathea. "Oh, He is the man who took the body of Jesus and laid Jesus in his own tomb."

We were delighted to solve the puzzle. "You are Christian?" they asked?

"Yes." I agreed.

"We are Muslim! We believe in Jesus too! He is a great prophet of Islam. We believe that he will return!" We were thrilled to share the commonality of our faiths with each other in this Holy place as well as our shared humanity.

I later learned that the Church of the Holy Sepulchre has different areas made up of different Christian denominations, all keeping up their own traditions to honor and sanctify this place, but the Muslims also have a part in preserving this holy place. Rather than let any of the denominations of these churches under one roof pridefully feel that they are more important than the other, the churches agreed that a Muslim family be entrusted with the keys of the Holy Sepulchre. For over 850 years, two Palestinian Muslim families have helped preserve the sanctity and peace of this holiest shrine of Christianity.

Maneuvering through the construction and the tractors, I made it through the remaining five stations of the Via Dolorosa in the Church of the Holy Sepulchre. The work being done to continue to carefully preserve the history of this place for future generations made me grateful for the thousands of years of history in this place and the generations that it has taken to pass forward this legacy of love. Jesus suffered and died here so that we could have life, good life.

When Jesus taught us to pray, "our Father" he was already looking to our adoption into the family of God by his work. Already we have life more than suffering. We can receive eternal life with eternal hope! Jesus' journey did not end here. After three days, he rose from the dead. He was seen by all the disciples and many others. He ascended into Heaven at the right hand of God the Father. By this we know that our forever home is with God. We know that when we pray, God hears us. We know that our sins are forgiven. Life is good!

Chapter 10: The Desert Blooms

The summer after I traveled to Israel, I was honored to be invited by the bride to an Arab wedding. "What should I wear?" I asked excitedly, feeling completely unprepared.

"Whatever you want!!" Mona proclaimed with a flourish and a bright, wide, welcoming smile. I should have enquired further. However, I had no idea what questions I should ask. This would be like traveling to Narnia! A whole unexpected world.

I had a favorite dress that I rarely had the chance to wear, but I felt so pretty in it. So, I was excited for a chance to dress up. Mostly, the excitement was for my former student, who, with this glittering personality, would be moving into a whole new stage of life.

Mona was shy and a little apprehensive when she first told me she would be getting married. Eyes shining with courage, Mona shared about the man that she would be marrying, and I could see her warmth and a little nervousness trying to imagine her new life.

Providentially, arranged marriage is not altogether new to me. I had become friends with the mom of one of my students years before, who told me her story. She had studied and built her career, and rather than the dating scene, she had asked her parents to select a husband for her. They had a beautiful family together with whom I had the joy of teaching and becoming acquainted. On the flip side, I had thrown several baby showers and a couple of wedding showers for students in my school in Texas for girls who, ready or not, life was about to change.

This was not like the latter. This was a culture of love and support for the next stage in life. "Mona," I smiled, "You are a treasure. Your family knows what a treasure you are. You are ready for this. Your family is with you, and I am so happy for you."

Relief and emotion spread across her face for a moment. She was excited to be engaged! Then I saw her draw together her composure. As a former costume designer, I eagerly scanned her favorite dress designs. She showed me a sparkling dress that she called "gray."

"No, you can't wear 'gray.'" I declared, "But if you call that silver, that is gorgeous!"

Then we got into hair. "I was thinking about these hairstyles." Mona shared.

I had never seen any of the Muslim girls' hair. "Can you show your hair at your wedding?" I asked with surprise.

"Of course!" She beamed. I could already see that this Arab Princess would shine so brilliantly!

Sometime later, Mona sent me the invitation and called me. "I want you to be there!" It would be only women. Like a wedding shower, she explained.

Following the instructions on the invitation, I arrived on time. This was my second mistake (after my dress). It would be hours before the party began, but I heard God's voice again, "Listen."

About 45 minutes later, women began slowly trickling in and gathering in groups. The women in the modest Arab dress that I had become accustomed to seeing, long, mostly dark-colored conservative dresses and hijabs covering the whole body except for hands, face, and toes. Occasionally, a burqa covered all but the eyes. Touches of elaboration of style with some beading around the face or bodice, a bit of color could be seen here and there.

Groups of women chittered happily around the room. A few looked inquisitively at my strange presence in my strange dress, sitting alone and listening. Mona's mom guided me into the inner sanctum to greet the bride. She had chosen silver, after all! Her long, wavy dark hair shone, adorned with a tiara, and her jewelry was accented with silver. Her hands and arms were painted with wavy designs of henna as dark as her hair. The transformation was glorious, and I reassured her of her incredible beauty and the beauty of the event that she and her mom and sisters had been working so hard on.

When I returned to the room, more women had arrived. Suddenly, the room changed, and the young girls started crowding into the restrooms. The older women began removing the outer garments to reveal such beautiful gowns as I had never seen before!

Sparkling attire, jewelry, and henna designs on hands.

The transformation continued as the girls emerged from the bathrooms with glittery makeup and sparkly jewels fixed on their cheeks and eyes. At the tables, bags opened as girls started fixing each other's hair! Some painted or glued on their nails, their lips vibrant, and their smiles and laughter more so.

The room had gone from dull, conservative, a study of extreme modesty, to bright and glorious feminine power. I was so underdressed! The desert had bloomed!

A few of my other students had arrived, and I was invited to join a former student, along with her mom and sister. The women continued to prepare for the revealing of the bride. I could write a book about the details of this event, but we ate and danced with the bride.

Each one of us danced with the bride and declared her ready for marriage.

Here, I had the rare opportunity to take a longer listening look into an Eastern culture.

Few women outside of this community get to see the feminine power. The support and love that these women have for each other. The community that holds each other up. I have heard so many terrible stories about Muslim treatment of women in the past, but to be fair, I have heard more of these terrible stories out of any other Western culture. Most stories that make it to Western ears will be when a culture goes wrong, when judgment and hate can belittle others and reaffirm our own culture as better than theirs.

I listened, and I heard goodness.

Chapter 11: The Road to Za'atari

When I traveled through Israel, all the foods I ate made me hum with happiness. They were so good! It was all so beautiful: fresh salads and breads, fish and meat, cheeses and honey. So, on my last day in Israel, I visited a spice shop in the Old City of Jerusalem.

The shopkeeper was marvelous! He was delighted that I love the flavors of the Holy Land. He told me the stories of cooking. I had only eaten from restaurants for the week and had no home cooking, so I did not know how to cook with this rainbow of colors and flavors. The names were difficult for my mind to hold on to during this short visit to the market.

The merchant guided me to taste dozens of wondrous spices and spice blends. When I left, I bought as much as I thought I could cram into my luggage. I wish I could have taken more home, but I left full of joy with my find.

One spice mix was my favorite. Over the next few months, I realized that this flavor was worth the whole trip, and I needed more! I would travel the world for za'atar. I put this on everything, and everything that I put za'atar on was amazing: eggs, avocado, bread, meat, salads!

I was planning a trip to Greece (and I seriously hoped I could find za'atar there). My pain in my relationship with my daughters still made my soul ache, but my Grandma Olive had taught me that when you are depressed, the best medicine is to serve someone else. Grandma was a psychiatric nurse by trade and always before her time in social-emotional wellness.

That spring, there had been a devastating earthquake in Turkey and Syria. For at least ten years, I have been praying for the Syrian refugees. For some reason, my heart ached for them. I remember their first winter and how bitterly cold it had been. I know they have suffered.

I had looked briefly in this direction, but I was not associated with any relief organizations and would need training. However, in my search, I stumbled upon an organization in Athens that gave travelers an opportunity to volunteer to help with refugees in Athens. So, following the advice that my wise grandmother had given long ago, I looked into it.

There were a number of projects that I could join. I could teach children English and could work with women to teach them empowering skills, arts education, and computer skills.

Sure, I could do something like this. How wonderful it is to get to meet people and hear their stories! But as I glanced through the destinations, I saw Jordan pop up.

I am not sure why Jordan stood out to me. I had said to myself once when I stood on the bank of the Jordan River in Israel, "What's over there? I want to go there." Also, I had a former student who was planning to move to Jordan. However, it may have been a leading of the Holy Spirit. So, I decided to kind of poke a stick at this idea and see if it was alive. I applied, and I was accepted to work with women in Amman, Jordan.

I honestly knew nothing about Jordan except that I saw it from a few meters across a murky stream called the Jordan River from

Israel. I was still unsure about my choice, so I prayed with my friend Sherry. After a day, I was sure that the Holy Spirit was urging me toward Jordan.

I decided to go with the flow of God, follow what the Spirit was doing, and join him in that. So, I surrendered my plans to Him to take the path of the unknown in obedience and faith. Not that I wasn't afraid. I did feel out of sorts, like I was walking into a pitch-dark room without any idea what was inside, but God reminded me to abide in faith, hope, and love.

So, I accepted the volunteer opportunity and bought a ticket to Jordan. Two days before my trip, I learned that I would not be going to the capital city Amman but to Al Mafraq.

After a quick web search on Al Mafraq, I found that the largest Syrian refugee camp in the world was here. I would be working with the Syrian refugees, after all. Za'atari Camp held 140,000 Syrian refugees supported near the town of Al Mafraq, with a population of 60,000 Jordanians.

Now, you may have caught it, but it took me a week to realize that my craving for za'atar had helped lead me to Za'atari Camp. The home I lived in was actually in Za'atari Village.

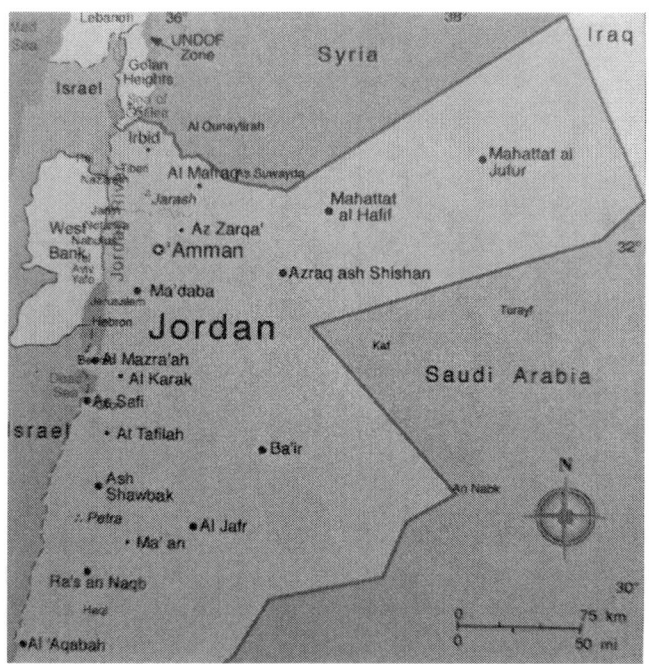

This was what I had been craving!

Chapter 12: Where is Jordan?

From San Francisco to Istanbul, there was a 12-hour flight, a layover in Istanbul, and then another flight from Istanbul to Amman, Jordan. The flight to Amman took a little longer than it should have. It was delayed, which made a few cranky travelers. One traveler in particular delayed the flight longer.

A man on the plane started arguing with the flight attendants, which further delayed the flight. The person next to me on the plane wore a beautiful blue hijab. She and I rolled our eyes at each other and looked to Heaven. "Pray for peace, right?" I typed into Google Translate.

"Na'am! Yes!" she nodded.

For the next couple of hours, I visited with this sweet grandmother and kindergarten teacher. She helped me with my Arabic, assuring me that I knew how to speak all of my polite words when I arrived in Jordan. I gained some good practice conversing using Google Translate as well.

We conversed about her recent trip to the States to visit her son and granddaughter in Chicago and my travels to Amman and Al Mafraq. After making our way through customs, we found each other again while we waited for our luggage. We visited a bit more and then left each other with gratitude for the peace and joy of spending time with a new friend.

My driver was from Al Maser, the organization from Amman, who would connect me with another organization from Al Mafraq. Wajeeh took me from the airport to my host family in

Amman. There, I would wait a day for another lady from Ireland, and we would travel together to work side by side in Al Mafraq.

On our short ride, Wajeeh told me a bit about the organization and how it had some inspiration for volunteer work from the King of Jordan. Wajeeh used to work with teens at an orphanage in Amman. These orphans were wards of the king himself. He would regularly check in with the orphanage and even play with the children. Wajeeh told me that the king claimed the children as his own, seeing to their needs and their higher-level education to prepare them for adulthood.

I marveled at this righteous act of godliness. I had often treasured the description of God from David in the Psalms: "A father of the fatherless, a defender of widows, Is God in His holy habitation." Psalms 68:5 NKJV

I arrived at my Amman host's home after 2 AM. However, they were happy to welcome me and to invite me to tea and conversation after I settled in. So, in the middle of the night, my host's eldest son, Zaid, shared his family's story with me. This family is Palestinian and has been in Jordan since 1948. While Jordan and Israel have a good treaty, this family cannot return to Israel even to visit without acknowledging Israel. This is difficult, but what do I know? I am Californian. I have no deep roots to land.

Zaid inquired about my plans for my free day the next day. He gave me some tips on what to see in Amman. So, after a few hours of rest, I slipped quietly out of the flat to explore Jordan.

Chapter 13: Bedouin Hospitality

I snuck out of my host family's place at 9 AM. Everyone was still asleep, but I had been awake since 5 AM. I napped, but by 7 AM, I was getting dressed and planning my day.

I really only had one firm destination and one loose plan, the Roman Theater and Uber.

I found the Roman Theater already quite warm by the time I got there. It was July and in the desert. I explored the theater, climbed to the top, and got a view of the city and perhaps another destination. I could see more Roman ruins at the top of the next hill. I explored the museum displays in the Theater that did not show Roman artifacts but Bedouin. Jordan is the home of the Bedouin culture.

I visited with the curator and the security guards about a path to the Roman ruins at the top of the hill, but it was getting very hot now as I crossed the courtyard. I would be climbing through a neighborhood up a steep set of steps. In the back of my mind, I wondered if I should just call an Uber rather than try to run the obstacle course of pickpockets and pushy guides. Nonetheless, I would at least have a look and a prayer about the start of this stair path up the hill.

On the way, several cabs were waiting, hopefully, to take tourists from the Roman Theater to other destinations. This was where I met Walid. When I inquired from him if he could take me to the Roman ruins at the top of the hill, he said, "Sure, no problem. It is a hot day." He spoke English easily, so we visited a bit.

He said, "Let me buy you a cup of tea." He bought me a sweet, hot mint tea and explained that it was a hot day. Bedouins know that when you need to cool down, drink something hot, and mint is also cooling. As we sat and visited, I don't know if it was the placebo effect, but I am inclined to believe that Bedouins know better about living in the heat of the desert than I do, and I felt quite comfortable.

Walid and I sat and discussed my trip to Jordan and this free day that I had in Amman. He gave me some suggestions on things I could do and see that day, suggesting he was available to drive me anywhere. We discussed a price to visit a few important sites in Amman, then head north to visit a Castle, the Jerash ruins, and lunch.

Walid turned out to be more than a driver or even a guide. He was an excellent teacher.

He helped me a bit with my Arabic, but mostly, he taught me about the culture of the Bedouin people and the culture of Jordan. In Amman, we visited the Blue Mosque and the Greek Orthodox Church, which were side by side. The church and Islam serve the people and God side by side in peace. Walid explained that Jordan was very proud of this. He told me some stories from Islam that I had never heard, but then he branched into the stories of Jordan.

The Blue Mosque is actually "King Abdullah I Mosque," and it was completed in the 1980s. Attached to it is a museum display of artifacts of Jordan and the Hashemite Monarchy. From this room you can access an assembly room from this room where the King makes public addresses to the elected representatives of the House of Representatives. It is notable that within this House of Representatives, 9 seats are reserved for Christians, 3 are reserved for Chechen and Circassian minorities, and 15 seats are guaranteed for women. I learned about Jordan's parliamentary system and how the King of Jordan is a father to his people.

This surprised me, because these elected representatives sounded remarkably like a democracy. I had always been told that Israel was the only Democracy in the Middle East.

As we then made our way north of Aman, Walid taught me about his own people. He was a Bedouin, raised in the desert in the south of Jordan. He explained much about living in the desert, the plants, the animals, amazing camel facts, and the camels whom he loved like they were family. He explained the styles of dress and many other customs.

Of course, my favorite customs are related to food. Walid took me to a restaurant that was like an oasis in the desert. Fresh flat bread cooked in a wood-fired oven, fresh sweetened mint and lemon juice, hummus, salads, olives, yogurt with dill, and shishkabob. The food never stopped coming, as the conversation flowed easily throughout the day.

What Walid taught me was mostly about the love for Jordan. The desert land is beautiful. He described the South, where he was from. The beautiful places in Wadi Rum and Petra.

His love for his mother and the things she and his grandmother taught him. His respect for his father and how he taught him hospitality. He taught him to listen to people first.

From there, he learned several languages and learned about many places around the world. He learned to share Jordanian customs with guests and to share a love for Jordan.

Jordan, at its heart, is Bedouin. At the heart of the Bedouin is hospitality and the love of guests. Jordan has a lot of guests, not just travelers like me. In addition to the 6.2 million people who are of Palestinian origin, Jordan hosts almost 800,000 refugees from many places, including Iraq, Yemen, Somalia, and Sudan, and 1.3 million refugees from Syria.

The generosity and hospitality of the Bedouin people in Jordan is stunning. How can a desert land carry such a load of suffering within its borders? Soon, I would see so much more in Al Mafraq, but Walid had tutored me in the culture and kindness of the people with whom I would live closely for the next two weeks.

Chapter 14: Sama Albadia; In the Desert

Wajeeh from Al Masar picked up Kate and me and drove us North into the desert, the Badia. We headed for Al Mafraq, which means "crossroads." Al Mafraq is a small city in the north of Jordan near the border of Syria with about 60,000 people. As we drove, Wajeeh told us more about our host.

Dina Alkhaldi spoke little English, and we spoke little Arabic, but we learned a bit more, and we communicated through Google Translate as necessary. Dina was the founder of an organization that serves the Syrian refugees at Za'atari Camp. The camp originally had over 100,000 refugees in 2011, but there are over 140,000 today because of births.

I recalled what I remembered about the Syrian crisis when I first learned that I would be going to Al Mafraq just a few days before. In 2011, a civil war broke out in Syria.

Families ran for their lives, but the borders were closed. To open the borders to Syrians was to risk war with Syria. I remember at the border of Jordan, young Jordanian men illegally crossing the border and dragging women and children to safety as the Syrian army approached. The following winter had devastating weather. The United Nations provided tents for the refugee camps, but the tents were inadequate for the harsh cold of that year.

The people were crying out for help. I have been praying for them ever since. As I looked at unrest around the world, I was always concerned and prayed for the displaced Syrian families.

I was amazed to learn that Dina and her family and friends volunteered to help these displaced people through various organizations for several years. In 2014, Dina founded Sama Albadia to meet the needs of the Za'atari refugee camp, which had been unmet by the United Nations or other government organizations. Kate and I would be serving the Syrian refugees through this organization in the areas of teaching children English and assisting in the Women's Empowerment Program.

When we arrived at the home of Dina Alkhaldi on the hot afternoon, she welcomed Kate and me into a beautiful, cool formal parlor where she served us tea and some sweets. We made our introductions, and I was very thankful for the months of Duolingo and the kind help from my friend on the plane and Walid, my tour guide, from the day before.

We talked about our experience. Kate was a science teacher from Ireland and soon to be teaching abroad in Dubai. I shared that I was also a science teacher in the States and a farmer with a degree in Plant Science. I had worked in vineyards and orchards and as an agricultural inspector for the Department of Agriculture in San Joaquin County.

"We are farmers," Dina replied happily. "Would you like to go to the farm?"

"Yes! This would be amazing!" I beamed with anticipation.

All through my drive through Israel and Jordan, I would look longingly at the farms, wanting to explore and tour the agriculture of the Holy Land. I was elated. We discussed the farm I grew up on with nuts and tree fruits and the huge garden that my dad kept, and we all worked at every chance we got.

Somehow, I felt so at home and so awkward and childlike. My life and my schedule were in the hands of Dina for the next two weeks, and I trusted her implicitly. So, Kate and I settled into our room, and we met in the family parlor for dinner. There, we met the rest of the family: Dina's mom, 'Mama', Dina's sister, Haya, Dina's brother and sister-in-law, and their two sons. We were treated to an amazing traditional dinner of Mansaf! This was new and wonderful, and so homey.

After dinner, I visited Mama and Haya for quite a while, sharing pictures from California and my time in Jordan with Walid the previous day. Haya spoke English, and she helped me visit with Mama. Suddenly, Dina popped into the room and indicated that we should hurry and follow her. So, without a way to question what we were up to, we obediently tagged along with our host. We slipped on our shoes and followed her to her car.

We drove to the edge of the village and out into the countryside. Dina pointed to the left and said, "Our farm." I could see a huge gate and rows of water trucks. Then she pointed to the right and said, "Zaatari Camp." I could see what looked like a sprawling city of trailers and streets and lights. We continued down a road till we hit a checkpoint.

Here, we could go no further. We stopped. The sun was setting, and the air was significantly cooler. Here, we got out of the car, and Dina began to explain using Google Translate that this was the edge of Za'atari Camp. 140,000 refugees live here, and the population has been growing because of births.

The camp was run on solar power, and the water for the camp came from her family's farm. Off to the right, children were playing football (soccer) on the open field. There were guards from the United Nations that kept those who did not have clearance to enter out and those who belonged to the camp in.

I asked if the guards were to protect them from the outside or to keep them in the camp.

"Both," Dina answered. The Syrian refugees would only get support from the government and the United Nations if they lived in the camp. If they left, they would need to support themselves, but they don't learn skills in the camp. She explained that Sama Albadia helps the refugees gain skills so that they can support themselves. Staying in the camp is not good. They lose hope if they are there for too long, and problems arise.

"The children do not have enough to do. Tomorrow, you will meet the children at the center and help them in their English class. If they speak English, they can get a job outside of the camp." Dina explained through Google Translate.

"I am so thankful to be here," I explained to her using the translation app. "I have been praying for the Syrian refugees for over ten years. My heart has broken for them, and I am amazed and honored to meet you and to serve you however I can."

Chapter 15: Weavers of Hope

Dina took me to the Sama Albadia community center early the next day and explained my tasks for the day. I would be teaching a supplemental summer English class to 10 to 12-year-old children. The children took English at school, but it was beneficial for them to work with a native speaker. Set up to do my lesson planning at the front desk, I had the amazing opportunity to practice my Arabic greetings with everyone who came in.

Everyone enjoyed a bit of conversation, and a few social volunteers helped me learn a few new words and their pronunciations.

Meanwhile, I worked on creating a fun lesson with the kids and asked volunteers for bits of help as needed. Volunteers moved cheerfully in and out in waves, sitting down for a bit of hot tea or Jordanian coffee as they waited for their activities.

The meeting rooms would be set up for training. Afterward, the volunteers would set up for another training. While other people would come in to sign up for something or to ask questions, drop off equipment, pick up something else… and the story goes. At the center of all the activity was Dina. She gave quick directions like a general but laughed joyfully. Everyone who came in felt loved like they were in their own home (but with a very strict mom!).

Dina came over and checked on my lesson plan, hummed, and nodded with approval. I am sure I beamed. Over the next week, I taught the kids some fun activities.

We sang some very American songs like "The Hokey Pokey" and "Old MacDonald." We played some games, and I told stories, but a lot of what we did was get down on our knees, eye level, with the kids sitting at the tables coloring, gluing, and listening to them tell us about themselves. They were just normal kids who loved to sing, draw, play games, and had visions of a future. Two little boys came up to me and told me that they were going to grow up to be translators.

In the afternoons, Kate and I joined several volunteers to go play soccer with the girls' soccer team. We met in a cracked parking lot behind some old buildings surrounded by weeds just a short walk from the Center. The coaches put the kids and me through the drills. Lectured them on important life skills, then we played several games.

On a nearby parking lot, the boys played. A coach came over and introduced himself to me. The coach explained that this opportunity for the girls was rare. The families had made a commitment that these girls would train together for the next six years to become a team that might one day play on a national girls' team. The vision of this program creates a spirit of incredible hope in these kids.

The second week, Kate had gone home to Ireland, but I got a surprise. Sixteen teachers from America on a Fulbright Scholarship were coming for a tour of Sama Albadia, and they wanted to teach an English lesson with me! So, we had an amazing day playing BINGO!

So many other programs came and went through the center, every day. I had no way to keep track of it all with my limited

Arabic skills, but nevertheless, I was able to greet people and share a few pictures with them from California or my lesson plans that I had for the kids. Programs at the center included addressing domestic violence, early marriage, and issues with the law. The center was in the process of starting a new program to address the social-emotional needs of the elderly. Women were organized in groups for economic empowerment to help them start small businesses to support their families.

Slowly, I learned that Sama Albadia serves the Syrian refugees by giving the Syrians the opportunity to serve themselves. They identify needs in the Za'atari Camp that are not met by the United Nations or by the Jordan government. Then, they devise a plan to meet these needs in the camp or among Syrians in the wider community.

I found the community Center delightful, with so many optimistic people coming together, men and women. In the middle, tightening all the strings and checking every detail, was Dina. As I listened to what was happening around me, a picture grew in my mind of a weaver, taking all these lives and all these needs and weaving them all together into something beautiful that gives great comfort and love to those in need.

My hope grew that I would be a small fiber, twisted into a strand and woven into a tapestry that delights God. This was a mission of hope.

I asked Haya, Dina's sister, if they were weavers. She said, "Yes! Our Mama! She is a weaver. How did you know?" I explained that the way Dina weaves people together at Sama Albadia is a beautiful creation.

Chapter 16: Learning to Listen

Listening is not automatic. It is a skill that I teach in school. So, as my blinders were removed, I began seeing what I had never seen before. When I learned to listen to Palestine, I began hearing what I had never heard before. My world was shaken. My mind on matters that I thought I knew was completely undone. I could have let myself be afraid of looking.

Instead, I chose to take my scientific philosophy that I say to my students all the time, "*I am wrong a lot, but it takes courage to be wrong.*" Being courageous to learn, I continued to listen, to pray, and to process. I was opening my heart and abandoning biases.

In Jordan, I took a few days to see the great sights of Petra and Wadi Rum. My guide was a Palestinian. His family had been in Jordan since 1948, but they held on to their identity as Palestinian.

He explained to me much about Jordan and the refugees that Jordan has accepted from Palestine, Syria, Iraq, Yemen, Somalia, and Sudan. When you include Palestine, nearly one-third of the population of Jordan are refugees. It is a remarkable country where the hospitality of the Bedouin people is the driving value, but there are heavy economic implications for the people of this country.

I learned that Jordan was at continual war with Israel from 1948 until 1994. Today's peace treaty is a good one that has offered much security to both Israel and Jordan.

Nonetheless, while Jordan is very proud that Christians and Muslims live side by side, Jews do not live here. There is a very quiet tension. The rulers of Jordan are careful of what they say. Jordan and Israel's cooperation had included projects that would have improved water supply to Jordan and hydroelectric power. These projects have not materialized.

When we got to Wadi Rum, we loaded into the back of trucks for a ride into the desert. I was given a spot in the back of a truck with four men. Using my polite Arabic words and Google Translate, we introduced ourselves.

These men were from Palestine. They proudly told me the names of their villages. Then I got to a tall man in the group. He was from Jenin. "Dude!" I said with respect. I held out my hand to take his hand in friendship. "I have heard a lot about Jenin in the news over the past few months. I pray for your people." I shared through Google Translate.

About this time, my guide was hopping in the back of the truck with us and started translating. He had worried that I would have trouble talking with these men. He explained that I was there to listen and that I was especially interested in Palestine.

They asked me if I had changed sides to support Palestine. As I hesitated, one said kindly, "No, that's okay. You do not have to answer."

"No, I want to answer." I explained, typing into Google Translate, "I am trying to learn to listen. I don't believe I deserve an opinion because how can I? Everything I thought I knew was wrong. Every time I meet someone, I learn something real. I am happy to meet you."

We had a wonderful conversation after this about what these men did. Two of them were farmers, with whom I enjoyed discussing agriculture immensely. We slid down some sand dunes together. Then we climbed a rock formation together. Sharing these recreation activities with these fellows who lived a world apart but were not that different was honestly meaningful.

Had I changed sides? Did I now favor Palestinians over the Israelis? My thinking had been wrong. Much of what I thought I knew was rocked. Except for God. I think of Joshua as he entered Canaan.

"When Joshua was by Jericho, he lifted his eyes and looked, and behold, a Man stood opposite him with His sword drawn in His hand. And Joshua went to Him and said to Him, "Are You for us or for our adversaries?"

He said, "No, but as Commander of the army of the LORD, I have now come." And Joshua fell on his face to the earth and worshiped, and said to Him, "What does my Lord say to His servant?

Then the Commander of the LORD's army said to Joshua, "Take your sandal off your foot, for the place where you stand is holy." And Joshua did so."

Joshua 5:13-15 NKJV

There is only one side, God's side. We are one race of people, one Father. We have one adversary, and the battle is the LORD's. I must learn to do what he says. For now, it is to listen.

Chapter 17: Taking Sides

I went to my first American football game this Fall. I attended Fresno State, Home of the Bulldogs, and the Red Wave. Fresno had some of the best fans in college football, but I wasn't among them. I lived across the street from Bulldog Stadium. Occasionally, I would go out on the patio to watch the fireworks after a touchdown, but I never actually made it into the stadium when I went to school there.

I am not the only Bulldog in the family. My brother-in-law, sister, and nephew are all Bulldogs too. So, while visiting my sister in San Diego, they decided to write this wrong of the universe and take me to a Fresno State vs. San Diego State game. Woof!

Before the game, my brother-in-law worked to right many wrongs, like my complete lack of understanding of football and a long-standing rivalry between Fresno State and San Diego State football teams. To prepare me to really understand the deep meaning of this game, Greg handed me a two-page article from the sports section of the San Diego Union Tribune. Then Greg quizzed me on what it said. It was full of statistics, strange lingo (what's a tight end?), and the "Old Oil Can" trophy. "Um... it says that Fresno is supposed to win?" I answered with no confidence.

"Good!" He went on to explain the ups and downs of the season for both teams. He turned back to the front page. "What is the Old Oil Can?" He asked, pointing to a particular paragraph.

I skimmed the section again, "It's a trophy."

"Right. It is only exchanged between these two schools." After a bit more explanation and getting me properly outfitted in red to join the Red Wave (San Diego confusingly wears the same colors), we made our way to the San Diego Snapdragon Stadium to cheer for Fresno State.

With the first touchdown to Fresno, our row cheered loudly, letting everyone around us know that we were the enemy. We felt the exhilaration run through us being on the winning side.

Soon, however, Fresno lost their lead. They fought back, but they never pulled back ahead. Our joy subsided. We moaned and groaned at the losses and the missed passes.

The funny thing is, we could have just changed teams. They lived in San Diego. We were wearing their colors, and our row won the fan appreciation prizes!! We each took home a bag of prizes that read San Diego Aztecs. Oh, and my nephew also caught a San Diego Aztec T-shirt from one of the cheerleaders.

It's just a game; we could have changed sides. Everything was there saying we should just experience the joy and change sides, but we are trained from young to take sides.

Belonging to something feels good, even if you are losing.

I thought back to my Palestinian friends that I met in Wadi Rum. They had eagerly asked me if I had changed sides. To change sides, does that mean that I needed to hate someone else?

I learned recently that the base for all propaganda is taking sides. Us versus them.

People in today's culture are well-trained for this.

The most dramatic and effective form of propaganda is dehumanization. If you can convince your target audience that the other side is less than human, you have a loyal following. The most prominent example is WWII Germany. Goebbels, the Nazi Minister of Propaganda, diligently dehumanized Jews. Without this action, the massive acts of genocide would not have been possible.

Now, this is NOT a political book. In fact, I believe that politics does not solve anything.

Politics are loaded with propaganda, dehumanization, hate, and fear. The pattern of political success is easy to see. Democrats accuse Republicans of some disgusting act, call them names, or characterize them as inhuman. Then, they ask for money so that they can defeat these hateful politicians. Republicans accuse Democrats of some disgusting act, call them names, or characterize them as inhuman. Then, they ask for money so that they can defeat these hateful politicians. Both sides keep doing this because it works. And the divide grows.

One can easily dehumanize Israelis by listing atrocities committed. One can easily dehumanize Palestinians by listing atrocities committed. However, we are human, one race. Desmond Tutu writes, "Let us condemn ghastly acts but let us never relinquish the hope that the doers of the most heinous deeds can and may change" (Tutu 57).

On a whole other perspective, my biology classes have students of every ethnic background and several languages. It surprises students to learn that biologically, there is only one race, the human race. (It has even been proven that

Neanderthals were not a different race but were, in fact, human, and we carry Neanderthal DNA, but that is a whole other story.)

One main goal in science is to listen to each other. The only way for science to move forward is to listen to each other because, inherently, in science, scientists are wrong a lot. Together, we test the strengths and weaknesses of every idea.

I often tell students that if someone tells you that science is about memorizing facts, they are lying to you. What we "know" from science is always changing. As we get new technology, new instruments for measuring or observing, new information from a scientific study or experiment, or an amazing new find, our body of "knowledge" changes. And it takes courage to be wrong.

The truth is that we all need to be on the same side. There is one race, the human race. We all need to listen to each other. Our goal should be to work together to give all of us the best outcome possible. Desmond Tutu writes, "I know in my heart that peace is possible. I know it is possible in your life, and I know it is possible in mine. I know it is possible for our children, our grandchildren, and the generations that follow...Peace is built with every small and large act of forgiveness" (Tutu 59).

Chapter 18: Stuck Between Two Psychopaths

I woke in the middle of the night, hearing a hard knock on the door. I have learned from the past that the knock is real (but not at the door), but only meant to wake me to start prayer. I immediately thought of praying for my Palestinian friends in Israel. I prayed for my daughters and for my friend battling cancer. Then, the Spirit brought me back to Israel. I prayed and then went back to sleep.

My mom called me that morning while I was reading my Bible and praying. She told me the war had begun in Israel. Hamas had attacked a peaceful event during the Holy Week of Sukkot. Hundreds were dead. Families decimated. Atrocities displayed the deranged minds of the Hamas attackers. Hate. A nation was in shock and in anger.

Authorities promised hate in return.

As I have watched this war unfolding, I think of an incident that happened to me and my friend last May as we were stuck between two psychopaths in a small space.

Last spring, my friend's son bought her and me tickets to see a Giant's Baseball game at Oracle Park in San Francisco for Mother's Day! We were treated to great seats and fantastic food, and we had an amazing time. However, on the way home, something frightening happened.

We were on a Bay Area train car. On the front end of the car was my friend's son, sitting with his girlfriend. Mary and I sat in the middle, visiting. We were happy about this amazing day, but her son had a lot to drink and was being rude. His mental health was fragile, so we were giving him space and enjoying ourselves. On the other end of the train car was a mentally ill man who was talking to himself. He was an African-American man who was ranting about racial injustice. A lot of people crowded on the train.

Everyone minded their own business, trying their best not to engage the lunatic. However, our host hollered across the car gruffly, "Hey man! Why don't you just keep it down."

Now, we all know that this is not going to calm or quiet anyone. This is an escalation.

Fighting words began being thrown back and forth across the car. Most people's eyes got big with whites showing, but they stared at their feet or hands. No one dared to say anything, as this thing escalated into waving hand gestures and violent words. Mary and I kept saying soothing words, "Rob, easy. Be calm. It doesn't matter. Rob, I love you; this has been such a good day."

He threw some threats at us. How dare we quiet him? He bought the tickets. He bought the food. Meanwhile, the other guy is still doing his bit of unstable ravings, now directed to engage and escalate Rob. The other passengers, full of terror on both sides, did their best to be small and unseen.

After this storm passed, Rob leaned over to his girlfriend, "You would never cross me like they did. That's what's wrong with this world. That guy needed the crap beat out of him. But you listen to me and do as you are told. You don't disrespect me like those two."

I was only glad that neither man was armed as we were stuck between two psychopaths. It was just words.

Tragically, in Israel and Palestine, the psychopaths are heavily armed. Mentally ill Hamas is engaging with mentally ill IDF. Innocent people between the two are the victims. Israel is a tiny country. No safe corner to cower exists to be out of the way of these warring, angry groups. Both groups are indeed suffering from the trauma of abuse. Then, as mentally ill people do, they inflict trauma and abuse on others. These innocent victims are inflicted with trauma and abuse, which potentially creates more people who, out of bitterness and fear, will inflict trauma and abuse on others. The fighting words, the escalation, and the violence help no one. Nothing will be resolved.

They need psychotherapy.

Some who dare to love will say some soothing words, and they will come under attack for their daring to be kind.

Yet, let me say some soothing words here. I am a high school teacher. I have to solve problems between over-emotional teens who do not trust me. I am a white lady.

Oftentimes, my African-American students do not trust me because I look like someone abusive toward them. At some point, when we just are not working well together, I will point at the door and say, "In the hall." These are fighting words for some. The hall is where they expect more abuse. They expect to be belittled, dehumanized and then threatened with punishment. I find this horrible.

This is what I do: "Lean against the wall. Stare that way." I tell them. Then I lean against the wall next to them, neither of us looking at the other.

"What, what do you want?" the student may ask as their frustration, fear, or anxiety grows, turning toward me.

"We are leaning against the wall until I calm down. Just lean." I will explain. Soon, I feel myself again. I am not answering the situation in anger, and the student is maybe becoming curious and more relaxed.

I look at the student and say, "I love you. That is my most important job, and I should not be here if I did not love you." This shocks and softens my student to the next thing that I offer. "We are not working well together, but we have a job to do. To give you the best life possible, we need to be on the same side."

At this point, I must be open to hearing the student. There is something wrong. Perhaps it was something that I said that triggered them. Perhaps it was simply because I looked like someone who hurt them in the past. Sometimes, students at this point will start telling me something very important that someone must know and care about for them to have a chance to succeed. The key is to convince them that I care, that I am on their side, and that there is only one side in my classroom.

Yohanna Katanacho put it this way from a Palestinian Christian perspective, "Any solution to the Arab Israeli conflict must take the mission of the land into consideration. Any political solutions must reflect justice, righteousness, and biblical love for both Palestinians and Israelis. It must empathize with the oppressed whether they are Palestinians or Israelis, Arabs or Jews" (Katanacho 43).

I am listening. I hear pain and fear and hate. I am not your teacher. I am just on a quest to listen, but someone needs to say to Palestine, Israel, Hamas, and IDF: We need to be on the same side.

There is only one race: the human race. I know there has been a lot of fear and pain. Unimaginable pain. Unimaginable trauma. We do not get better.

We do not heal from this if we do not heal together.

"To treat anyone as if they were less than human, less than a brother or a sister, no matter what they have done, is to contravene the very laws of our humanity. And those who shred the web of interconnectedness cannot escape the consequences of their actions." Desmund Tutu from *The Book of Forgiving* (19).

Chapter 19: "Olive You!"

My grandmother was named after a tree, "Olive." "Olive Darling Pond." Her favorite joke was:

"Knock knock.

Who's there?

Olive.

Olive who?

Olive you!"

That was my grandmother. She loved us and taught us to love. She was a psychiatric nurse by trade, so she was before her time addressing the emotional wellness of her family. Sitting at her knee and working by her side, I learned many things. (I will tell more about Grandma Olive later.)

My other grandmother was named "Grace," but she also loved trees. She had two old olive trees, but they were important trees in our lives. We played under them, climbed them, and every fall, Grandma made home-cured olives. The olives are part of our family tradition of flavors. Grandma Grace cured the olives with lye and then brined them with salt. Easy… but when she was old, my dad took over.

Olives are extremely astringent. They are inedible off the tree. So, my dad would cure the olives with lye in a five-gallon bucket out in the shop, and I was always right by his side learning the steps.

He picked the olives green, then soaked them in water with lye (sodium hydroxide) for 2-3 days with a plate on top and a brick on top of the plate to make sure the olives stayed submerged. They were ready for the next step when he cut them and could see the lye had worked its way all the way to the pit. The clear water turns black during this curing stage.

Next is the rinsing stage. All those black tannins and the lye must be rinsed out. Dad would drain the olives, rinse them, and soak them in fresh water. By the next day, the water would be black. So, he would drain and rinse the olives and refill with fresh water. Dad would do this for three to five days until the water would stay clear.

The next test was a taste test. If the olive tasted at all "soapy," he would keep on rinsing. If the olive tasted good and creamy, it was time to add the salt brine. Dad would add just the right amount of salt into the water and cover the olives with a salt brine for a day. We would taste the olives each day until the salt was perfect. Then they were ready.

I have a friend, Issa, a Palestinian Christian from Bethlehem. Issa recalls that the olive harvest was the best time of the year! Students would be let out of school to help with the harvest. The kids would work the high branches. They would cook amazing food out under the trees. It was family time, where the whole family worked, played, and ate together.

Children learned about the trees from their families. They would learn that many of the trees were hundreds of years old. They had been cared for by family throughout the year. Protected from harm. Planted by ancestors generations before.

Every year, the family would work the harvest together out under the trees.

I had hoped to join my friends from Jordan in the olive harvest this year. Mama, the matriarch of the family, Dina, her daughter, and my host were so excited to share their love for their family and farm with me last summer. The farm had tomatoes, peppers, eggplant, okra, melons, squash, sunflowers, and acres of olive trees. Most importantly, it had a family.

Every time we went out to the farm, family members were out to greet and to show their love for the land. Children would run down the rows, showing me an eggplant or a tomato and teaching me Arabic names. It was summer, so usually, we went out just before sunset as the desert air was cooling.

Mama invited me back to join the olive harvest, so I quickly bought a plane ticket! This is an amazing time of the year for the whole family to gather, work, and celebrate the harvest. Mama and her family of 11 children and their families with kids ranging from 4 to late teens (and one newborn baby girl!). This is a time when the connection between the family and the land is bonded and celebrated. Joy, family, laughter, children, parents, grandparents, aunts and uncles, cousins, food, hard work, and the great reward of the year, the finest olive oil in the world comes from this region of the world.

These resilient trees, many hundreds of years old, endured drought, extreme heat, and cold. They have nourished families for generations. Olives trees are the pride of the land.

This year, the bombardment of Gaza has been shocking. Reluctantly, I canceled my plans to go to Jordan. I wondered what was happening with the olive harvest in Palestine. I am shocked and so stricken by grief by what I have learned.

It is not yet possible to know how much of the olive harvest of 2023 is lost, but the situation is bleak. About 25% of the Palestinian economy comes from olives. Most olive groves are not being harvested because of war. Many, many trees are being destroyed, bulldozed, or set on fire. What has wrenched my heart more, this is not new to 2023.

The United Nations Conference on Trade and Development reported in 2012 that 800,000 productive olive trees were uprooted in Gaza and the West Bank between 1967 and 2012 (Buxbaum and Yacoub). In the last 11 years, this has intensified. Many more orchards have been bulldozed, burned, or even sprayed with herbicides. Caring for the trees has become dangerous in areas near Israeli settlers. In one case, a Palestinian family was attacked during the harvest, killing one.

The current conflict is even involving olive trees in Lebanon. Israel has been firing white phosphorus artillery shells into the orchards of Lebanon, destroying 40,000 acres of trees. Hundreds of Lebanese farmers have been displaced and their livelihoods ruined (Pedrazzi).

As I look at these attacks on the land, I can't help but think of the display of Solomon's wisdom in I Kings 3. Two mothers come before Solomon. The women lived together, but one child had died. They argued before the King who was the mother of the living child and who was the mother of the dead child. Finally, Solomon called for a sword.

"And the king said, 'Divide the living child in two, and give half to the one and half to the other.' Then the woman whose son was alive said to the king, because her heart yearned for her son, 'Oh, my lord, give her the living child, and by no means put him to death.' But the other said, 'He shall be neither mine nor yours; divide him.' Then the king answered and said, 'Give the living child to the first woman, and by no means put him to death; she is his mother.' And all Israel heard of the judgment that the king had rendered, and they stood in awe of the king because they perceived that the wisdom of God was in him to do justice." I Kings 3 25-28 NKJV

God is wise and just. As these trees are destroyed, as the land is destroyed, as bombs and poisons of war pollute the land, I wonder how God will judge. I think of Jesus' words from the sermon of the Beatitudes, "Blessed are the meek, for they will inherit the earth." Matthew 5:5 NKJV

"With every olive tree that gets burnt, uprooted, and vandalized, a wider truth emerges: there is one side that claims the land as its own by protecting it and lovingly looking after it, and another side that claims it as its own by destroying the nature and eradicating its agricultural history." (Pedrazzi).

The long-living, slow-growing, resilient olive trees have another meaning to the people of the Middle East and to the world. They are a symbol of peace. You may have heard the phrase "extending an olive branch." This phrase effectively means to end the conflict between two parties.

Another symbol of the olive tree is a man stretching out his arms to heaven in prayer. This seems so fitting as Jesus taught his disciples to pray on the Mount of Olives in Jerusalem.

My Grandmother Olive used to say that she didn't like her name until she grew old and learned that "Olive" meant "Peace." Then she loved her name and her joke: "Olive You."

Chapter 20: The Bottom-Line Weekend

Saturday morning, I got an urgent call from my mom. I needed to get to the hospital in Tracy. My dad had surgery three days before, but he had an incident in the hospital. This was serious. So, as I was rushing to be with him, I sent a message to my Palestinian friend.

"Do you have time to pray for me? My dad has been in the ICU for three days. I am heading to the hospital now. He had some sort of episode."

"Sure. Sorry to hear that; I will pray for him for sure."

Then, I got a text from another friend. My good friend Keri, who had been battling cancer, died that morning. I was weeping and unable to go forward or back. I just leaned over and wept. I don't know how long I sobbed. I keened. This horrible cry would just burst out of me. I had to go, but I was devastated already.

I reached out to my friend again. "...only prayer helps in these circumstances." He answered as he assured me of his prayers. So, I stuffed in my emotions, grabbed my things, and headed for the hospital.

Along the way, I decided to reach for strength and encouragement from Christian radio.

Here is what I heard:

The National Crawford Roundtable

The Bottom Line Episode 217:

Saturday, October 14, 2023

Speaker 4: *"If I was Israel, I would carpet bomb the entire… I would give them "x" amount of time to leave. I would carpet bomb the entire place, dozer it over and start over and not let 'em back in. That's what I would do."*

Speaker 1: *"Actually, that's kinda what Bibi Netanyahu said that they were going to do."*

Speaker 4: *"That's what I would do."*

Speaker 1: *"They unleashed it."*

Speaker 4: *"Yep, that's what I would do."*

Speaker 1: *"You know what's a shame of this is, John? I get what you're saying here, and I would fully- well, I am conflicted- part of me says you want a proportional response. The other part says that the only way you handle terrorists is to eradicate them."*

Speaker 4: *"You aren't going to handle it any other way than do it the way I just said. If you come up with some sort of a treaty, a ceasefire, a whatever, this is coming back again."*

Speaker 4: *"They've allowed this garbage to go on. There's the Dome of the Rock on the Temple Mount. Just end it. Be done with it."*

Speaker 1: *"I know. And that means that they need overwhelming force that they need to completely decimate Gaza. And yes, that does include women and children, and that's a really difficult thing, but it's a necessary evil."*

Speaker 1:" *I think taking a squeegee to Gaza, as horrific as that sounds, to do this and decimating it and turning it into complete ash and rubble that does send a message to Iran and Hezbollah and Hamas and the rest of the terrorists and you know what? Do not mess with us."*

Speaker 4: *"We as a country (the USA) need to be in full support of whatever they do along those lines."*

I was not encouraged. Instead, I felt a devastating blow. People of my faith, in my country, were broadcasting, advocating for the genocide of a people on National Radio.

This is not the heart of God. This is Hamas. This is the IDF. This is insanity.

I turned it off, crying out to God. Praying out loud for the people of Gaza. For the people caught between the insanity of hate. I prayed for my dad. I prayed for Keri and her family. I knew in my heart that I would lose him that day, but I still could not imagine, even seeing it before me, how we could survive such pain.

Likewise, I could not imagine how people in Gaza could survive the pain of losing so much. Everyone who died would face such fear and pain. Everyone who survived would lose family. Everyone who survived would be faced with fear and bitterness.

How their souls would ache.

When I got to the hospital, I met my sister and my mom. Dad had coded. His heart had stopped, and they were working on bringing him back. "Please," we asked the doctor, "can mom go in with him? He needs to hear her voice." The doctor agreed, and

Laura and I stood outside the room praying. This happened three more times.

My body started going into shock. My body shook, and my teeth chattered. While this happened, my Palestinian friend reassured me of his prayers in texts. In the end, all the doctors left as my father passed into eternity. Laura, my mom, and I prayed and sang to my dad.

My dad passed to his heavenly father in peace. Over the next few weeks of funerals, family gathering together, asset management, and support from family, friends, and our church, my mom and I often related our deep devastation of losing my father to the unimaginable pain in Gaza, the West Bank, and Israel.

While we were trying to make order in our small bit of chaos, the IDF was carrying out what the Christian Radio program had been predicting, decimating Gaza and turning it into complete ash and rubble. Thousands of innocents were dead.

Chapter 21: Switch

Sitting in the funeral home, my mom, sister, and I waited for the funeral director to return with the big book of prices. Our emotions swayed from gipping grief to numbness like the waves on a shore, but we took comfort in being together to make decisions with such support from our community and to mourn together.

As we waited in this moment of numbness, like that quiet moment when the waves recede back into the sea, my phone pinged. It was a news report. I groaned. "What is it?" my mom asked.

"Israel has bombed The Baptist Hospital in Gaza," I answered.

"Oh no!" Laura groaned.

So, as we waited together to bury our father, we felt such sadness for the people in Gaza who would not mourn their dead with the support we now had. Their loss would be so much greater. Their loss would be so unjust: the deaths of people who had so much to look forward to, who had committed no wrong, and hospital staff who were there to heal and serve people. We prayed for the people in the terror of that moment, for which we could not relate. My mom, sister, and I prayed together for the lives in Gaza, for the pain and grief of loss.

Later, the Israeli government spun the narrative to try to convince the world that Hamas bombed the hospital by accident. Some sort of clumsiness or incompetence.

Now, I do not have satellite capacity or some other type of superintelligence to determine if this was true or not, but President Biden appeared to be convinced that Hamas was to blame. On the other hand, and this is far more significant, Israel has not hesitated to bomb any hospital, church, or school since this incident.

America, after all, did not back off the unconditional support of Israel even after this event, the next school bombing, church bombing, subsequent hospitals, and the list continues to grow without any accountability for the extreme devastation to innocent victims.

That evening, my Palestinian friend called from Nazareth to check on me. I was surprised at how joyful he sounded. "How can you be so cheerful?" I asked. "You have bombing to the North of you in Lebanon and horrible devastation in the South in Gaza?"

"Lani," he explained, "When you are Palestinian, you have to learn to 'switch.' You must look at what is happening, and when you can take no more, you switch your eyes back to the LORD. The hope and the joy are still there."

After sharing this with my mom and sister, we practiced this often. As it felt too difficult to move on, we would read from the Bible, stop and pray together, put on some praise music, or just praise the LORD.

My Palestinian friend was right. The hope and the joy were still there. I found I had phrases that I would turn to for encouragement and repeat often. "I trust you, God." "This is God's story, not mine." "Praise God." "Praise the LORD." "Praise God in everything." "This is the best thing that could have happened. I just don't know why yet." "God uses everything for good." and "Life is good."

Also, I have some favorite hymns and songs that I would sing or play. "How great is my God," "Awesome God," and "In Jesus' Name," just to name a few. These songs affirmed my faith and where my strength to carry on came from.

The next week, a student asked me, "Ms. Lanchester, how do you keep smiling?!" My dad had died less than a week ago, but I continued to teach my lab classes. I explained to her about my Palestinian friend teaching me that when the pain is really tough, I can switch my eyes back on Jesus, and my hope and joy are still there.

Yohanna Katanacho, an ordained Palestinian minister, explains, "Palestinians are able to escape the tsunami of depression by means of the hope of resurrection - not only the resurrection of the historical Christ but also the resurrection of a divine eschatological reality in which there is hope in a just and good God. This hope is found in the Gospel, which communicates a message of life rather than destruction and death, and in the Church, which may seem to be dwindling and weak, yet is like yeast in dough. Its power is not measured by its size but by its significance." (Katancho 61).

I listen to the resilience and strength of the people of Gaza. The people of Gaza have been stuck between Hamas and the IDF for decades now. They have taken brutal losses even before October 7, 2023. The people are constantly rebuilding, treating wounds, and recovering. How do the Palestinians cope with such trauma that, if not currently happening, it is looming in the future? I can see how, as my Palestinian friend and Yohanna have said, it is about switching our focus onto our Christian hope, but what about the Muslims?

As I watched the video footage from Gaza over the last few weeks, I could see that these people had hope and resiliency, but I needed to understand Arabic to understand it.

Sadly, the Arabic that most Westerners are familiar with, we see as threats and violence.

In Western media, villains are often Allahu-Akbar-screaming terrorists.

To hear Palestinians, I had to understand what these terms actually mean. "Allah" simply means God in a general sort of way, as Christians say, "Oh God."

"Allah Akbar!" This simply means God is the greatest. It is often said when people are happy. Or "Alhamdulillah" means all praise to God. These are reaffirmations of their hope. It is often said in gratitude to God, as Christians would say, "Thank God."

As I watch the videos, people are crying out in pain and fear, "Allah! Allah!" Some are sweetly saying, "Allah Akbar!" as a child is pulled alive out of the rubble. Some are saying "Alhamdulillah!" as they struggle with pain, and help arrives.

These sayings are not fearful weapons but declarations of faith. I do not hear the people of Gaza as weaponized individuals but people of family, of culture, and of faith. I see the violence inflicted. The pain and the horror of violence in any culture is when things have gone wrong.

In a Bible study group this fall, a lady vehemently insisted that God does not hear a prayer to "Allah." As I learn to listen to these videos from Gaza, I relate the cries of pain and the calls to Allah as a call for hope out of despair.

I believe, and tremble, that God hears the cry of the Palestinians.

Chapter 22: The God Who Sees, the Who God Hears

My brain had become foggy and confused after my dad died. My normal, highly competent self was struggling to keep up at work and even with household business.

I cried out to God aloud. "You say in your word that my tears are precious to you, but I don't understand! How can I hear your voice through my tears? How can it be good for me to not hear you?!" I begged for him to send someone to speak aloud for him.

An hour later, a friend of mine from a local church stopped by. We had met before in the neighborhood, and I had made her coffee that I had brought home from Jordan. She knew about my plans for going back to Jordan that fall for the Olive harvest, but I had not seen her since my dad died, the war in Gaza, and this fog had set into my brain. I had reluctantly canceled my travel plans.

I was giving in to the fog. In my sorrow, I found my brain was only partially functional. I seemed to be running on short-term memory only. I can barely remember those days.

My work was suffering. I had a difficult time keeping up with answering the needs of my students and other teachers. I was just so tired. If I stopped, I cried or fell asleep. My mom and sister were the same. This was difficult when we would disagree on what we had decided earlier or done earlier. It also made making any decisions at all difficult.

So, I hit "pause" and did not go to Jordan.

I was so grateful that my friend stopped by. I spilled all this out to her. She and I prayed together for God's peace and direction. We prayed for Gaza. We prayed for Keri's family. We thanked God for my dad's life and his entering his forever home with God in Heaven.

As we prayed, I heard God's voice. His care and his kindness were all there. His reassurance and gentle voice conveyed this message to me: "You need to carry grief and the overcoming of bitterness to go where I have for you to go."

God saw me.

The God who sees. This is one of the names of God from the Old Testament. I found out that the only woman to name God was Hagar. Hagar, the slave woman who bore Abram a son, but while she was still pregnant, she had been abused by Sarai and neglected by Abram.

It must have been a great distress to run away into the wilderness while pregnant! God saw Hagar, and he affirmed her value. The angel of the LORD found Hagar.

After giving her instructions to return to Sarai, He blessed her: *"Behold, you are with child, and you shall bear a son. You shall call his name Ishmael because the LORD has heard your affliction. He shall be a wild man; His hand shall be against every man, and every man's hand against him. And he shall dwell in the presence of all his brethren."* Genesis 16:11-12 NKJV

The term "wild man" from this translation is the onager, a wild donkey. How can being a donkey be a blessing? Well, Hagar was a slave. The onagers are a type of donkey, a wild donkey that cannot be domesticated.

They are free donkeys, not slave donkeys. They are nomads. In Job 39:5, God himself, in his monologue to Job, characterizes the wild donkey that is referred to in this promise.

"Who set the wild donkey free? Who loosed the bonds of the onager?" Just as God would later see the affliction of the Israelites in bondage in Egypt, God saw the affliction of Hagar in bondage under Sarai.

So, the promise to Hagar is that Ishmael will be free.

But there is another beautiful promise hidden in this blessing; the angel of the LORD names Hagar's son "Ishmael," which means "God will hear." This future tense of the verb in Ishmael's name indicates that the promise is for her son, who is yet to be born. God has seen Hagar, and he will hear Ishmael.

So, when will He hear Ishmael? In Genesis 21, Ishmael is probably in his early to mid-teens. God has changed Sarai to Sarah, and she has a child. Sarah decides Ishmael will not share the inheritance of Abraham's household. What a shock to Abraham when he turns to God, and God tells Abraham to do as Sarah says. Abraham sets Hagar free.

Ishmael receives no inheritance from Abraham. He only gave Hagar a skin of water and some bread, not even a camel.

When I was living with Dina's family in Jordan in July, the afternoons were incredibly hot. Around 2-5 PM, everyone is inside. The desert did an amazing thing in the afternoon. As the heat builds up on the desert floor, currents of hot air rise up into the air. This swirls with the less hot air higher up. Along with this rising stream of heat, the air picks up sand and dust. As you look across the landscape, you can see dozens of these towering, swirling dust devils. The air becomes hazy brown. You definitely do not want to be outside without a head covering.

Mama and I would spend this time in the parlor together. We would take a nap in the heat of the day or play with the children, drawing or telling stories. This was not a time to be out without shelter. I imagine this was the time of the day that Hagar and Ishmael found great distress.

The Bible tells in Genesis 21 that Hagar left Ishmael under some shrubs and walked away to another location about a bow shot away. She was sure they were about to die, but in verse 17: *"And God heard the voice of the lad."* (not Hagar, but Ishmael)

God continues, *"Fear not, for God has heard the voice of the lad where he is. Arise, lift up the lad, and hold him with your hand, for I will make him a great nation. Then God opened her eyes, and she saw a well of water. And she went and filled the skin with water and gave the lad a drink. So, God was with the lad; and he grew and dwelt in the wilderness and became an archer. He dwelt in the Wilderness of Paran, and his mother took a wife for him from the land of Egypt."*

God heard Ishmael as promised. Ishmael was not without inheritance, but the inheritance came from the hand of God. God was with the lad. Ishmael goes on to be the great Patriarch of the Arab nations.

Growing up studying the Bible from a Zionist perspective, I missed so much. With my blinders removed, I can clearly read that Abraham and Hagar raised Ishmael to know and serve God. Hagar had seen the Angel of the LORD and named God, אֵל רֳאִי, the-God-who-sees-me. Then, in their need, God hears Ishmael.

The Arab Nations come from the blessing of God.

God hears Ishmael.

As I listen to Palestine, I see the distress as more than 40,000 Palestinians have been killed. So many people are crying out to God in their distress. So many children have died. So many children have become fatherless. So many women have died. So many women are widowed. I pray to God the Father to the fatherless and the defender of widows, the-one-who-sees-me, to the God who hears.

God hears Palestine.

Chapter 23: A Lesson in Humanity

Standing in line in the grocery store, an old homeless man was dumping out change and crumpled dirty bills on the counter. Next to the dirty money was a new, clean blanket from the discount rack in the back of the store. His white and gray hair was matted, and his beard was scraggly and stained. He wore a heavy army jacket, but last night had been cold, and this night would be colder. Long, filthy nails pushed money around the counter. He was frustratingly slow trying to count money to buy the blanket.

Two clerks rolled their eyes at each other, exasperated and just wanting to get him back outside so they could clean the counter.

I heard God speak to me, *"Pay for the blanket."* Feeling shy, I reached for my wallet but hesitated for just a moment.

At that moment, another clerk tapped me on the shoulder, took my basket, and said, "Follow me." I did. I rushed through my checkout, being polite, and I thought, *I will find the man and see how I can help him,* but he was gone.

I followed man instead of God. In that moment, a man was dehumanized, treated like refuse to be cleaned up. Was his need met? Maybe he got the blanket, but either way, he would be sleeping on the street, and who would know his name? Who would offer him kindness or mercy?

The lesson was a quick moment in my life that has replayed over and over in my mind.

So many things I learned about myself, about people, and my relationship with God.

I find it so automatic and easy to follow humans who politely say follow me. They will accept me and tell me that I have followed the right path. I have allowed them the space to clean up a mess. I have not injected my hand into a situation that was none of my business. In fact, I partnered, in my passive way, with dehumanizing a man whom God created and loved.

I hesitate to follow God, questioning my mind, my resources, and the abilities that God has given me to obey him. I often say, in hard things, "I trust God." In the little subtle things, I need to learn to hear God's voice and obey him quickly. The hesitation, the moment of doubt, gave room for a temptation to present itself.

I chose to follow the man. I am trained in politeness and in passivity to follow human direction instead of God.

God is a radical! He will make me into a radical! He would have me jump in and change the life of a man. He would have me see him as a human. He would have me know that God sees and loves him. He would have me see that this man is of immeasurable worth. He would have me love him.

I also learned from the clerks. They did not see a man; they saw a problem. They saw filth, refuse, inconvenience, frustration, embarrassment, but not a human.

It was the Holy Spirit that helped me recognize the mess before me as a man whom God loved. It was the Holy Spirit who helped me to relate my own soul stuck in a pit to this man stuck on the street. Over the next year, the Holy Spirit would bring back this moment and teach me about dehumanization.

Dehumanization is the denial of full humanity in others, along with the cruelty and suffering that accompany it. A practical definition refers to it as the viewing and the treatment of other people as though they lack the mental capacities that are commonly attributed to human beings. (Wikipedia)

It was shocking once my eyes were opened to dehumanization. It is everywhere and must be deliberately named and scrubbed out. This is the real insidious filth of the situation at the checkout counter. It is like a transmittable disease. In fact, it started in the Garden of Eden. The very first dehumanization was of Eve by Adam.

Then the man said, "The woman whom You gave to be with me, she gave me of the tree, and I ate." Genesis 3:12 NKJV

After the fall is discovered by God, Adam seems to have forgotten Eve's name and her relationship with himself. He calls her a most detestable name, according to my Grandmother Olive. My grandmother was a psychiatric nurse. She saw the most detestable slur not to be a four-letter word but a three-letter word.

While standing right there next to him, Adam calls Eve "she." "She' is standing right here!" my grandmother would say. "'She' has a name!" Grandma would emphatically point out. If I ever dared call my mom or my sister or her "She" in their presence, I would be swiftly corrected.

Adam seemed to have forgotten Eve's name. He forgot that just the day before:

And Adam said:

"This *is* now bone of my bones

And flesh of my flesh;

She shall be called Woman,

Because she was taken out of Man." Gen 2:23 NKJV

If there had been a bus, Adam would have thrown Eve under it. Now, to be fair, the first time the name "Eve" is in scripture is Genesis 3:20. After God has a talking-to to Adam, Eve, and the serpent. Then curses and promises are distributed, and then Adam calls his wife's name, Eve. Nonetheless, Adam denies the very special relationship that he has with "the woman." Yesterday, Eve was bone of my bone and flesh of my flesh.

Adam says we are part of each other. He adores her. The next day he points his finger and says, the woman, "She" did it. At that moment, he denies that they are the same.

Eve has been dehumanized.

I also make the point about "she" for two reasons: I love my grandmother and everything she ever taught me about mental health. The second is that she taught me that names are important. Our names are a gift from our parents. It is a gift of humanity. When you learn someone's name, you humanize them. You link them back to that gift of love and human experience.

I once had a high school student whose nickname was "Poopy." As I was learning my students' names that year, he informed me of his nickname. He didn't like his real name because people had mocked him that it sounded "black" (but they used a rude term). He didn't want me to call him by that name. I informed him that he was nearly 18 and that I would not disrespect him with such an insulting nickname.

I explained that he had a beautiful first name and that it was a beautiful gift from his mother, but if he did not like it, I would call him by his surname. After calling him Mr. Thompson for several months, my student told me that he thought about his name and my affirmation of it and started going by his name. We humanize each other by learning each other's names and affirming their value.

Learning names in my classroom has been more challenging these last several years.

About half of the students in my class have Arabic names. Now, some of these names are very easy for me to learn and pronounce. With others, I have been a dismal failure. It is because there are sounds in the Arabic language that are so different than English, especially for my laid-back California English. This is why I started studying Arabic, just to pronounce my students' names. This humanizing connection was well worth my effort. The connection that we make by just learning someone's name can be profoundly touching.

On the other hand, the incident at the checkout counter has shaped an awareness of dehumanization. I have learned that injustice starts with dehumanization. The war in Gaza between Hamas and the IDF is full of dehumanization. Both sides called the other animals in the beginning.

I don't even know what to say. As I have begun listening to Palestine, I listen to IDF raids in Palestinian villages, the Israeli settlers' attacks on Palestinian communities, and the number of children in military prisons; I am bewildered. The dehumanization of the Palestinian people is nightmarish.

Over the last year, I have been reading accounts of children's arrests from Palestinian villages. Because these children are detained by military detention and are tried by military courts, these children as young as 12 may be incarcerated in inhumane conditions for up to 9 months without trial.

Parents accept plea deals because a trial may take more than two years, and a plea deal would shorten their term. Usually, the charge is stone-throwing. The children who accept a plea deal are coerced into naming others who also threw stones as part of the plea. Some children are said to be completely innocent. Not only are they losing months to years of their childhood, but they are also losing their innocence and their peace. Why is this happening? Because they have been dehumanized, not loved as children, but labeled as terrorists.

The IDF has employed an AI (artificial intelligence) system to create targets for bombing. Nightly, the IDF is dropping hundreds of bombs on "targets." Each of these targets is killing innocent people. Nightly, the casualty rate goes up, and more innocents are trapped beneath the rubble.

I am offended that the name of this AI system that creates "targets" is named the "Gospel." The true gospel came to the rescue and saved the lost. I am convinced as a Christian that the true meaning of the Gospel should be made known in Israel.

The dehumanization of both the Palestinians and the Israelis is thick and is spreading through the nations. As people take sides, they would have you see the other side as monsters, dehumanized and worthy of death. However, as I put this before the LORD, the truth is simple, profound, and more powerful than all the weapons being thrown at each other together.

As a Christian, I will promote love and forgiveness and denounce genocide. The Bible shows me that this is the way.

On the cross, Jesus forgave those who killed him. As Stephen was stoned, he forgave. As Jesus' followers were slain, they promoted love and forgiveness, not hate and fear. This is why the church grew.

The Gazans are beloved by God. The Israelis are beloved by God. Jesus came to die for their salvation. I recognize that I am a fragile, vulnerable, flawed human being capable of thoughtlessness and cruelty. My life is a great mixture of goodness, beauty, cruelty, heartbreak, indifference, love, and so much more. I cannot divide the good from the bad, the saint and the sinner. This is our shared human nature (Tutu 125).

Jesus has shown me that the true power of humanity is revealed when we unleash the power of unconditional love. This is how to create an environment for positive change. That is the good news of the Gospel.

Chapter 24: Forgiveness and Overcoming Bitterness

"Then Abraham breathed his last and died in a good old age, an old man and full of years, and was gathered to his people. And his sons Isaac and Ishmael buried him in the cave of Machpelah." Genesis 25:8-9 NKJV

There are so many things that I can say about the conflict between Israel and Palestine.

But in the end, I listen, and I hear God. I hear hope that two nations that started as brothers will once again be one family. This is God's plan. Jesus taught us to pray "Our Father." At the end of Abraham's life, Isaac and Ishmael demonstrate that they were brothers with one father.

Jesus came to restore this peace between God and mankind. My daughters still have not talked to me in over a year. Even with the death of my father, the Papa who they loved so dearly, we remain estranged. I love them so much. I yearn for their company and friendship. They are my two favorite people in the world, and nothing changes that. Yet, I cannot imagine how God yearns for those estranged from him.

Jesus taught us to call him "Abba, Father" because God the Father sees us as his children. He created us for a relationship with him, and he is crazy about us!

I like the way Jesus tells it. *"The Son of Man has come to save that which was lost.*

What do you think? If a man has a hundred sheep, and one of them goes astray, does he not leave the ninety-nine and go to the mountains to seek the one that is straying?

And if he should find it, assuredly, I say to you, he rejoices more over that sheep than over the ninety-nine that did not go astray. Even so, it is not the will of your Father who is in heaven that one of these little ones should perish."

God demonstrates unconditional love for humans. Each person is a precious creation by God's own hand made in his image. A human being is someone of infinite worth because a human being represents God, and it goes for everybody!

I listen and I hear God. We are one family. These are my amazing brothers and sisters.

Isaac and Ishmael demonstrated, in the end, that they were brothers, but can Palestinians and Israelis ever be brothers? The Book of Forgiveness by Desmond Tutu has been a close companion to me in this journey. I look at Gaza right now and wonder how we come back from this. It is crushing. We need to change the environment.

Kia Scherr, who lost her husband and daughter in a terrorist attack in Mumbai, explains, "I knew the only way I could go on living was to forgive the terrorists. In those moments, I knew that forgiveness was essential, so I forgave…I knew that to respond with love to an act of terror was the only way to triumph over terrorism."

She goes on to explain the result of her act of forgiveness, "Forgiveness has allowed me to keep my heart open and soft. I chose to forgive because I knew that if I did not, the unforgiving would have kept me closed and hardened inside... This is true transformation. When we unleash the power of unconditional love, we create an environment for positive change. There is still a world of possibility even when the worst thing happens that could possible happen." (as cited in Tutu and Tutu 123-124)

In reading this Book of Forgiveness, I explored our shared humanity. We all have good and bad qualities. I will not go further here because I really believe that reading the book is an essential need at this point. Forgiveness is not easy. Forgiveness is not a weakness. It takes hard work. It needs a guide. Here is the Four Fold Path described in the book:

1. Telling the story

2. Naming the hurt

3. Granting forgiveness (recognizing shared humanity)

4. Renewing or releasing the relationship (Tutu and Tutu 49)

I listen and hear God. We are all one nation. Jesus taught that when we pray, we pray to God, "Your kingdom come, your will be done on earth as it is in heaven." In Heaven, there is only one King, which means there is only one nation.

I am inspired by the work of Desmond Tutu and all of South Africa. This nation was torn into so many fractions of hate, violence, and oppression that it would seem that there was no possibility to recover. However, they made forgiveness a national project.

Together, they listened to each other. Through the path of forgiveness, they brought peace to South Africa. When Palestine and Israel do the same, they will be a light of peace to all nations.

When I listen to Palestine, I see decades of trauma and dehumanization that have made the Palestinian people rely on God. I hear prayer and people seeking to do the will of God, our creator, our king. I hear faith, hope, and charity.

Most importantly, there is love.

I will end with a Palestinian voice. Yohanna Katanacho shares his Palestinian prayer inspired by Psalm 87, which should be the prayer of all.

"O Lord, you have given birth to a whole nation in Zion. There, you destroyed all forms of vengeance. You have given birth to the civilization of love and turned foes into friends. Rahab, Baylon, Philistia, and the children of Israel acknowledge that you are the Lord of peace. There are no ethnic barriers or bigotry. Evil has run away. It has become a transient shadow in a dream. An inclusive civilization has been born, one that includes sisters as well as brothers. It has no place for evildoers. After a long season of war, murder, and hatred, a feast of love has been born. Jesus is the seed of the new creation, and through him, Zion is filled with songs and praises.

We don't want only the birth of souls but also the birth and embodiment of the civilization of our dreams. The kingdom of God is righteousness, love, and all sorts of peace. O Lord, won't you make Zion a lighthouse in every corner of the world? Won't you imprison Satan and his fiery arrows? Let there be no more killing, or wars, or hatred, or bigotry. I will not stop dreaming! O Lord, bless your church! Let her move forward by your grace and strength" (Katanacho 87).

Appendix

Chapter 1

Al Tahhan, Zena. "Shireen Abu Akleh." Al Jazeera, 11 May 2022,

https://www.aljazeera.com/news/2022/5/11/shireen-abu-akleh-israeli-forces-kill-al-jazeera-journalist. Accessed 15 November 2023.

Berger, Miriam. "Analysis | U.S. response remains muted a year after slaying of reporter in West Bank." Washington Post, 10 May 2023,

https://www.washingtonpost.com/world/2023/05/10/us-response-remains-mutedyear-after-slaying-reporter-west-bank/. Accessed 15 November 2023.

Chapter 2

Bajec, Alessandra. "How Palestinian Christians are being driven out of Jerusalem." The New Arab, 13 January 2022,

https://www.newarab.com/analysis/how-palestinian-christians-are-being-driven-out-jerusalem. Accessed 15 November 2023.

HAMS, MAHMUD. "Israel's apartheid against Palestinians." Amnesty International, 1 February 2022,

https://www.amnesty.org/en/latest/campaigns/2022/02/israels-system-of-apartheid/. Accessed 15 November 2023.

Mallinder, Lorraine. "Under Israeli attack: Who are the Christians of Gaza?" Al Jazeera, 1 November 2023,

https://www.aljazeera.com/news/2023/11/1/under-israeli-attack-who-are-the-christians-of-gaza. Accessed 15 November 2023.

Chapter 3

Lawler, Andrew. "Jewish Extremists' Attacks Rattle Christians in Holy Land." National Geographic, 22 September 2021,

https://www.nationalgeographic.com/history/article/151224-israel-jewish-terrorism-arson-christian-church-multiplication?loggedin=true&rnd=1700078533910. Accessed 15 November 2023.

Berger, Yotam, Nir Hasson. "53 Mosques and Churches Vandalized in Israel Since 2009, but Only 9 Indictments Filed - Israel News." Haaretz, 24 September 2017,

https://www.haaretz.com/israel-news/2017-09-24/ty-article/53-mosques-churches-vandalized-in-israel-only-9-indictments-filed/0000017f-e101-d9aa-afff-f9595b9f0000. Accessed 15 November 2023.

"Joseph of Palestine- July 22 (Everyday Saints Series) | Theresa Zoe Williams."

Patheos, 22 July 2020,

https://www.patheos.com/blogs/contemplatioculture/2020/07/joseph-of-palestine-july-22-everyday-saints-series/. Accessed 15 November 2023.

Chapter 4

Cook, Jonathan. "Why Israel has silenced the 1948 story of Nazareth's survival." Mondoweiss, 12 January 2016,

https://mondoweiss.net/2016/01/silenced-nazareths-survival/. Accessed 16 November 2023.

Hatuqa, Dalia, and Neve Gordon. "The Nakba: Five Palestinian towns massacred 75 years ago." Al Jazeera, 15 May 2023,

https://www.aljazeera.com/news/2023/5/15/the-nakba-five-palestinian-towns-massacred-75-years-ago. Accessed 18 December 2023.

Kaylor, Brian. 2021. "A Ceasefire Won't Bring Peace to Gaza. Only Justice Will." Word&Way.

https://wordandway.org/2021/05/21/a-ceasefire-wont-bring-peace-to-gaza-only-justice-will/.

Kaylor, Brian, and Steven R. Harmon. 2015. "Baptists from Nazareth Appeal to Global Baptists at Congress." Good Faith Media.

https://goodfaithmedia.org/baptists-from-nazareth-appeal-to-global-baptists-at-congress-cms-22820/.

Pappe, Ilan. Ten Myths About Israel. Verso Books, 2017.

Tubb, Ed, and Mitch Potter. "The Toronto man who saved Nazareth." Toronto Star, 20 December 2015,

https://www.thestar.com/news/insight/the-toronto-man-who-saved-nazareth/article_d07daec6-4159-5b2c-81be-68850de4b35e.html. Accessed 16 November 2023.

Chapter 6

Al Tahhan, Zena. "The Naksa: How Israel occupied the whole of Palestine in 1967 | Features."

Al Jazeera, 4 June 2018,

https://www.aljazeera.com/features/2018/6/4/the-naksa-how-israel-occupied-the-whole-of-palestine-in-1967. Accessed 16 November 2023.

Davis, Warren. "Who Will Stand for Palestinian Christians?" *The American Conservative*, 4 October 2023, https://www.theamericanconservative.com/who-will-stand-for-palestinian-christians/. Accessed 26 May 2024.

Eldar, Akiva. "Will 1967 Palestinian refugees ever return?" Al-Monitor, 22 September 2016,

https://www.al-monitor.com/originals/2016/09/israel-palestinians-uprooted-in-1967-ignored.html. Accessed 16 November 2023.

"KAIROS PALESTINE." Kairos Palestine, 15 December 2009,

https://www.kairospalestine.ps/sites/default/files/English.pdf. Accessed 2 December 2023.

"Palestinian Refugee Camps-Bethlehem." Bethlehem Gate,

https://www.bethlehem.ps/en/Article/133/palestinian-refugee-camps. Accessed 16 November 2023.

Chapter 12

Andoni, Lamis. "Jordan is not Palestine | News." Al Jazeera, 4 July 2010,

https://www.aljazeera.com/news/2010/7/4/jordan-is-not-palestine. Accessed 23 November 2023.

"Refugees and migrant health country profile: Jordan - Jordan." ReliefWeb, 17 March 2023,

https://reliefweb.int/report/jordan/refugees-and-migrant-health-country-profile-jordan. Accessed 23 November 2023.

Chapter 13

Sama Al Badia Charity Association | Civil Society Organizations in Jordan,

http://www.civilsociety-jo.net/en/organization/22039/sama-al-badia-charity-association. Accessed 24 November 2023.

"Meet Deena Alkhald." Women's Peace and Humanitarian Fund,

https://wphfund.org/deena-alkhald/. Accessed 24 November 2023.

"MINISTER OF SOCIAL DEVELOPMENT VISITS UN WOMENS RESILIENCE AND EMPOWERMENT CENTERS." UN Women Jordan, 10 May 2018,

https://jordan.unwomen.org/en/news/stories/2018/may/minister-of-social-development-visits-un-womens-resilience-and-empowerment-centers. Accessed 24 November 2023.

"Rana believes that building trust and relationships are essential to succeed."

Norwegian Refugee Council (NRC),

https://www.nrc.no/career/career-stories/rana-salem/. Accessed 24 November 2023.

Chapter 15

"Data on casualties | United Nations Office for the Coordination of Humanitarian Affairs - occupied Palestinian territory." OCHA oPt,

https://www.ochaopt.org/data/casualties. Accessed 18 December 2023.

"Jordan vs. Israel." Peace Research Center Prague,

https://www.prcprague.cz/fcdataset/jordan-israel. Accessed 18 December 2023

Chapter 16

Katanacho, Yohanna. The Land of Christ A Palestinian Cry. Eugene, OR, Pickwick Publications, 2013.

"Ten Ways to Fight Hate: A Community Response Guide." Southern Poverty Law Center, 14 August 2017,

https://www.splcenter.org/20170814/ten-ways-fight-hate-community-response-guide. Accessed 16 November 2023.

Tutu, Desmond, and Mpho Tutu. The Book of Forgiving: The Fourfold Path for Healing Ourselves and Our World. Edited by Douglas Carlton Abrams, HarperCollins, 2015.

Chapter 17

".". - YouTube, 2 October 2022,

https://www.listennotes.com/podcasts/the-bottom-line/101223-the-national-crawford-YTX3WpUCGIZ/. Accessed 16 November 2023.

Chapter 18

Katanacho, Yohanna. The Land of Christ: A Palestinian Cry. Wipf & Stock Publishers, 2013.

"Timeline: Israel's attacks on Gaza since 2005 | Israel-Palestine conflict News." Al Jazeera, 7 August 2022,

https://www.aljazeera.com/news/2022/8/7/timeline-israels-attacks-on-gaza-since2005. Accessed 17 December 2023.

Mansour, Bader. "The Baptist Hospital in Gaza: between 1954 and 1982." Come and See the Christian Website from Nazareth, 18 October 2023,

https://www.comeandsee.com/view.php?sid=1427&fbclid=IwAR1TYhb7hnmcXNa5pBT4wWXxzd-AC_V2fxXviLdYgQSR4h-rKlgO0Ox9gRM. Accessed 20 December 2023.

Chapter 20

"Dehumanization." Wikipedia, https://en.wikipedia.org/wiki/Dehumanization. Accessed 10 December 2023.

2023, March, IDF ". העדכונים, הכתבות, הנתונים והתיעודים | את"צ." Force Defense Israeli

https://www.idf.il/%D7%90%D7%AA%D7%A8%D7%99-%D7%99%D7%97%D7%99%D7%93%D7%95%D7%AA/%D7%99%D7%95%D7%9E%D7%9F-%D7%94%D7%9E%D7%9C%D7%97%D7%9E%D7%94/. Accessed 10 December 2023.

Karanth, Sanjana. "Israeli Defense Minister: 'We Are Fighting Human Animals.'"

HuffPost, 9 October 2023,

https://www.huffpost.com/entry/israel-defense-minister-human-animals-gaza-palestine_n_6524220ae4b09f4b8d412e0a. Accessed 10 December 2023.

"Number of Palestinian Children in Israeli detention | Defense for Children."

DCI-Palestine, https://www.dci-palestine.org/children_in_israeli_detention. Accessed 10 December 2023.

"UN: Over 200 Palestinians, nearly 30 Israelis killed in 2023." NY1, 21 August 2023,

https://ny1.com/nyc/all-boroughs/international/2023/08/21/this-year-over-200-

palestinians-and-nearly-30-israelis-have-been-killed--highest-since-2005--un-says. Accessed 10 December 2023.

"Why are so many Palestinian prisoners in Israeli jails?" Al Jazeera, 8 October 2023,

https://www.aljazeera.com/news/2023/10/8/why-are-so-many-palestinian-prisoners-in-israeli-jails. Accessed 10 December 2023.

Chapter 21

Tutu, Desmond, and Mpho Tutu. The Book of Forgiving: The Fourfold Path for Healing Ourselves and Our World. Edited by Douglas Carlton Abrams, HarperCollins, 2015.

Chapter 22

Al Jazeera. "'Our hearts burn': Gaza's olive farmers say Israel war destroys harvest." Al Jazeera, 6 November 2023,

https://www.aljazeera.com/features/2023/11/6/our-hearts-burn-gazas-olive-farmers-say-israel-war-destroys-harvest. Accessed 14 November 2023.

Brunet, Emad, director. 5 Broken Cameras. Guy DVD Productions, 2011.

Buxbaum, Jessica, and Hala Yacoub. "How Israel enables environmental terrorism in the West Bank." The New Arab, 14 November 2023, https://www.newarab.com/features/how-israel-enables-environmental-terrorism-west-bank. Accessed 14 November 2023.

Hedroug, Layla. "Israel's Campaign Against Palestinian Olive Trees – The Yale Review of International Studies." The Yale Review of International Studies, 11 March 2023,

http://yris.yira.org/global-issue/6018. Accessed 14 November 2023.

Ibrahim, Noor. "Why the West Bank Olive Harvest Is a Flashpoint for Conflict." Time, 1 November 2019, https://time.com/5714146/olive-harvest-west-bank/. Accessed 14

November 2023.

Pedrazzi, S. "In the West Bank, Israeli Settlers Are Burning Palestinians' Olive Trees." Jacobin, 10 November 2023,

https://jacobin.com/2023/11/west-bank-israeli-settlers-palestinian-olive-trees-violence-occupation. Accessed 18 December 2023.

Chapter 23

Katanacho, Yohanna. Praying Through the Psalms. Langham Global Library, 2018.

Tutu, Desmond, and Mpho Tutu. The Book of Forgiving: The Fourfold Path for Healing Ourselves and Our World. Edited by Douglas Carlton Abrams, HarperCollins, 2015